EFRÉN HERNÁNDEZ
A Poet Discovered

EFRÉN HERNÁNDEZ
A Poet Discovered

MARY M. HARMON

UNIVERSITY AND COLLEGE PRESS OF MISSISSIPPI
HATTIESBURG

Library of Congress Catalog Card Number 72–76854
International Standard Book Number 0–87805–012–4

THIS BOOK IS AUTHORIZED
AND SPONSORED BY
THE UNIVERSITY OF SOUTHERN MISSISSIPPI

PREFACE

EFRÉN HERNÁNDEZ, a young man of twenty-four years when he first appeared on the literary scene, grew to manhood during one of the most turbulent periods of Mexican history. In the political, social, religious, and cultural spheres, the country had been shaken to its very foundations in an upheaval that left its mark upon the people, the institutions, and the literature.

At the beginning of the Revolution, in 1910, Mexico was already experiencing another revolution, this one of a cultural nature. The intellectual youth were revolting against a sterility that had grown out of modernism and post modernism and out of positivism, which in Mexico had been converted into a pedagogic movement. They were turning toward a simpler, more human, and, in their view, a more American form of expression. Intellectual maturity was the professed aim of the new movement, and it was around the literary magazine, *Savia moderna*, that the group, el Ateneo de Juventud, was formed. This autodidactic assembly was composed mainly of essayists, philosophers, and humanists. Numbered, also, among them were such poets as Luis G. Urbina and Enrique González Martínez.

López Velarde, often named the finest poet of the epoch, was not a member. In his desire for change, he was more interested in renovation of content than of form. He concerned himself with the *intimidad* of Mexico and, turning away from the city, with its noise, violence, and sin, retreated to the provinces to wander, a solitary spirit and a Wordsworth gone ironic.

Authors of the revolutionary period had presented the sad reality of the Mexican situation in a naturalistic and realistic manner. They were often careless of language and technique. Opposed to this lack of attention to detail, a new sensibility was to develop in the work of the Ateneo, some of whom, influenced by the pastoral tendencies of Velarde, took refuge in their provincial past. Others of the group began to set a new course, choosing between the two aspects of what was now labeled the Vanguard: the Contemporáneos and the Estridentistas. It was the Vanguard that brought Mexico back into touch with *lo universal* and awoke the interest of the Western world, especially that of France, in Mexican letters.

The first group took its name from its outstanding literary review, *El Contemporáneo* (1928–31). Inwardly oriented, *hacia adentro*, and avidly seeking after culture, its members turned their eyes toward contemporary France, somewhat less toward other continental countries, and toward England and America. The Estridentistas, less intellectual, oriented *hacia afuera*, wanted to break all the old norms, to destroy the past, to look only towards the future, to construct and perfect a completely new esthetic. Their interests lay more in the political and social spheres than in the cultural, and it was from various European ideologies—Italian futurism, Spanish ultraism, French dadaism—that they received their greatest inspiration. Their frantic literary activism was, perhaps, a necessary explosion, but one that produced little of lasting value.

Such was the intellectual climate prevailing when Efrén

Hernández first claimed attention in the field of letters. Many of his closest friends, among them Alejandro Gómez Arias, Andrés Henestrosa, Octavio Novaro, and Salazar Mallén, were shortly to form the nucleus of the so-called Generation of 29. Although contemporary with this generation, Hernández was in reality not one with any literary school. Rather, he had his own literary bent, one founded primarily on the blending of the work of the classical Spanish writers with local traditions and folklore.

Although an increased interest in literature has emerged in Mexico during the past twenty years, there is still lacking a vigorous discipline of literary criticism. The novel seems to have reached its belated high point, having finally become the most popular of the genres and the short story and the poem continue to maintain their public appeal. Even so, essayists—especially those who concentrate on literary matter—command small attention. Many friends of Hernández, and some scholars, have expressed in newspaper and magazine articles their disappointment that the work of Hernández has not been justly appreciated. Soon after the writer's death, in 1958, Antonio Rius Facius expressed the hope that this work of such positive quality might soon be collected, carefully edited, and published. José Tiquet has marveled that, in spite of the magnitude of Hernández's work, so little, in point of fact, has been said of it. Marco Antonio Millán, emphasizing the deep tenderness, the simple wisdom, the sad beauty, and subtle *humorismo* of the work of Hernández, has lamented that the arbitors of literary taste have not accorded it greater esteem. M. Hernández, characterizing the author's literary production as one of great originality—"*producto de una de las más auténticas vocaciones que se han dado entre nosotros*"—has bemoaned the fact that it has not yet been the subject of a profound study.

In 1965, Hernández's outstanding works were, for the first

time, collected and published in a volume entitled *Obras: Poesía, novela, cuentos.* Among his private papers are some yet unpublished works. His essays on theories of art and literature and on his plays, a small number of his poems, and some examples of his prose have been published in newspapers and periodicals. It is in these sources, also, that one finds most of the criticism of Hernández's work. In 1963, Teresa Bosque Lastra presented "La obra de Efrén Hernández" [1] as her *tesis para Maestría* at the Universidad Iberoamericana in Mexico City. In this valuable thesis she has compiled many pertinent facts concerning Hernández and his work: a short biography, the names and publication dates of his writings, brief discussions of his style and of the various genres which he cultivated, personal data furnished by his family, notes on the unpublished works loaned to her by the family, and a concise bibliography.

Hernández's name, along with sketchy criticism, is beginning to appear in histories of Mexican and of Latin American literature. The critics, however, as critics will, generally disagree about the value and even the nature of his work. For example, Enrique Anderson Imbert includes the oneiric novel of Hernández among the poetic narrations of the Contemporáneos, naming him with Torres Bodet and Gilberto Owen as the "narrators more subjective than objective." [2] And Teresa Bosque Lastra, agreeing with the opinions of several other critics, maintains that the similarity lies only in the fact that the poetic narrations of each one have fantasy as their base. Luis Leal asserts that Hernández is closer to the Ateneístas than to the Contemporáneos. Octavio Busta-

---

[1] Teresa Bosque Lastra, "La obra de Efrén Hernández," Master's thesis, Universidad Iberoamericana, 1963.

[2] Enrique Anderson Imbert, *Historia de la literatura hispano-americana,* Vol. II: *Época contemporánea,* 1st ed. (Mexico City: Fondo de Cultura Económica, 1961). This work serves as a source for the generalizations of this preface.

mente classifies the novel *Cerrazón sobre Nicomaco* as a surrealist tragedy, a classification dramatically at odds with Hernández's own ideas about surrealism. (Hernández stated that he could never accept the validity of surrealism because, concerning it, no two opinions coincide, a fact which not only renders impossible any terse definition, but which, by a rather tenuous logic, also, condemns the movement itself on the grounds that "la verdad es única, sólo la mentira es infinitamente variable.")

This book will deal with Hernández as he is revealed through his biographical data; his stated and implied philosophy; his poetry; novels; and, to some extent, his stories. It leaves for later attention a detailed scrutiny of a number of his short stories. Final judgment—if there be any such event—must be deferred until the man's works have attracted more universal attention. I aim, however, to set out, via sympathetic comprehension of Hernández and his literary achievement, toward an evaluation of the man's work and toward an expected modification of our histories of Mexican—perhaps of modern occidental—literature.

The substance of this study derives from my thesis, "Appraisal of Efrén Hernández, A Mexican Thinker," which was written in 1969 under the able direction of Professor Eduardo Scheel at the University of Southern Mississippi. Many people have assisted with both the original study and this revision. I wish here to express my gratitude to Miss Teresa Bosque Lastra, Mrs. Efrén Hernández (wife of the poet), Miss Valentina and Mr. Martín Hernández (children of the poet), and Professors Roger B. Johnson, Jr., and Eduardo Scheel.

MARY M. HARMON

Hattiesburg, 1972

CONTENTS

EFRÉN HERNÁNDEZ
A Poet Discovered

Chapter I

TESTIMONIES TO THE MAN AND WRITER

Efrén Hernández, the second son of Efrén Hernández and Josefa Hernández de Hernández, was born September 1, 1904, in the small town of León, in the state of Guanajuato. In this provincial spot he was to spend many of his formative years and was to receive both his primary and secondary education. It was during these years that he began to write poems and to demonstrate an unusual interest in literature. In his "Ficha biográfica" he wrote:

Mi afición a la literatura, creo yo, es heredada. Más de cuatro parientes míos, de la generación de mis padres, hicieron versos. He aquí, como ilustración, unos muy breves, debidos a Efrén Hernández, el viejo:

"Bien sé que el triste acento que el náufrago envía
de la distante playa do el viento lo arrojó,
destemplará los tiernos acordes de alegría
con que sus plectros de oro te brinda la ilusión.

"Y sé también que quiso sus íntimos pesares
dejar en el olvido y despertar su fe,
y enviarte el entusiasta cantar de sus cantares,
más dulce que las notas de idílico rabel.

"Mas ya cuando el santuario del alma se convierte
en ruinas bajo el beso amargo del pesar,

3

> las liras enmudecen y al soplo de la muerte
> la luz de la esperanza se apaga en el altar." [1]

He seems to have loved, admired, and respected his father, but it is apparent that his feeling for his mother was far stronger. It was to her that he owed his Indian heritage as well as, he believed, his highly developed imaginative faculty.

> ¿Qué importaba que mi padre supiese hablar francés, inglés, griego o latín, ni que entendiera ciencias y ejercitase artes, si no juntara a estos estudios la capacidad de ver el corazón? ¿Y qué mi madre escribiera sin ortografía, si estaba siempre próxima y su tacto percibía las formas de las almas? [2]

Surely his lifelong Pascalian struggle between the head and the heart must have grown out of this early divergence of influences.

The death of his father, in 1918, left the family in straitened circumstances and was a source of bitterness and shock to the fourteen-year-old son, who from then on was forced to face life on his own. After having served a short apprenticeship in a pharmacy, he became a *mozo* in the same court in which his father had been a judge. Later he was apprenticed to a shoemaker, then to a silversmith. In the meantime he was studying at home, preparing for the examination by which he would gain the "título de suficiencia" from the secondary school in León. In accord with his late father's desire that Efrén follow in his professional footsteps, the young man traveled to Mexico City, where he enrolled in the Facultad de Derecho in the national university of Mexico. He never moved away from the city.

---

[1] Efrén Hernández, *Obras: Poesía, novela, cuentos,* ed. by Luis Mario Schneider, "Letras Mexicanas" (Mexico City: Fondo de Cultura Económica, 1965), 3. In the novel, *La paloma, el sótano y la torre,* the father of the protagonist, Catito, is credited with having written this poem (*Ibid.,* 206).

[2] *Ibid.,* 113.

Among Hernández's close friends at the university was Dante Ponzanelli, who was later to become his brother-in-law. Through this friendship, Hernández came to meet and, later, to love Ponzanelli's sister, Beatriz. Both socially and materially the status of the Ponzanelli family was much higher than that of Hernández, with the consequence that Beatriz's family looked with some disfavor upon the alliance. In spite of her family's objections, however, Beatriz was married to Efrén in 1937; and until his death she was his loving wife, his companion, and according to one commentator the inspiring muse of his lyric writings "de carácter amatorio." [3] From this union came two children, Martín and Valentina.

Although completely dedicated to a literary career, Hernández was forced by economic necessity to undertake work foreign to his nature. In his "Ficha biográfica" he explained that he had "worked at everything." After having been a book salesman he installed a plastics workshop and from time to time augmented his income by making earrings and other baubles of plastic, as well as lanterns with broken glass and tin of fantastic colors. He even sold little plaster figures in the *Lagunilla* ("market place"). For a short while he tried selling corn on commission. (One thinks of the poverty-stricken Cervantes, who managed storehouses of wheat.) This highly sensitive artist was condemned, further, to play the role of *petit foncionnaire*. It was this employment, however, which supplied him with the very meager livelihood that made life at all possible. The whole of his adult life was, in fact, a struggle both economically and physically. (In this struggle he brings to mind Hart Crane, his contemporary and fellow sufferer under the economic lash.) Always poor, at times near destitution, "reasonable poverty" had

---

[3] M. Hernández, "Reinventario de la producción hernandina," *El Libro y el Pueblo*, IV (September, 1963), 8.

for Hernández a curious appeal. The numerous portrayals of his alter ego—the protagonists of his short stories and novels—always experience the poverty he endured. In describing the protagonist in the short story, "Un escritor muy bien agradecido," Hernández wrote that "he would have liked to have enough money to eat supper from time to time, to have a coat in good condition, with elegant, wide lapels." But hidden under the writer's ostensibly vulnerable capacity for feeling, was a steely sense of pride and honor, which enabled him to confront his life with courage.

His student days were spent in a drab room on the Calle del Carmen, near the Zócalo (main square of Mexico City). Even this relative squalor could not be sustained, and he and his family moved repeatedly, seeking a manageable economic level. During the last years of his life they lived in an aged house of provincial character on the Calle Luis G. Vieyra, number 69. For this house he himself made all the furnishings.

On occasion, Hernández loaned his services to the Instituto Nacional de Bellas Artes. In 1942 he and his friend, Rubén Salazar Mallén, founded *América*, a little magazine that became signally important. The poet attained considerable power in *América*, and his works appeared periodically in it under the pseudonym, Till Ealling—a name which, considering the picaresque and *humorístico* tone of much of this work, may well have been chosen as a play on the name of the German practical joker, Till Eulenspiegel.

Throughout his adult life he had suffered from stomach trouble. His health continued to deteriorate; and on January 28, 1958, he died of a heart attack. His living, according to one of his friends, seems almost to have been a continuous dying. Two days later *El Zócalo* announced: "Efrén Hernández triumphed. He fulfilled himself. . . . His work, as pure as his life, should endure." [4] Many of his friends, who thought that his true worth had been unappreciated by the public during his lifetime, expressed their feelings at his death. Antonio Rius Facius wrote in *Excelsior* that his death was reported in the newspapers in a little column hidden in a corner, that it was only the unimportant ones who found important positions. He added that the silence concerning the writer's death was in keeping with the silence he had sought throughout his life and that, without "tumultos mentirosos," he had returned to the earth.[5]

If the manner of his life and death was beset by grim poverty and sickness, Hernández's physical appearance was likewise far from suggesting the cliché of the ethereal poet. María Luisa Mendoza called attention to the contradiction between his personality and his physical appearance.[6] Indeed, it was remarked often enough that his exterior form mocked his interior, his spiritual beauty.[7]

Ricardo Cortés Tamayo described him as a pale, nervous man with "a large mustache meticulously shaped like two wide wings above his lips, which were imperceptibly ironic and on which from time to time one might glimpse disenchantment and deception." [8] Elena Poniatowska saw him as "slender and dried up, with the skin stretched over his cheekbones like that of a chicken on a spit." She was impressed by his gentle expression, his large, nervous hands, which seemed always to be knitting an invisible sweater,

---

[4] "Fue sepultado ayer el gran prosista mexicano, Efrén Hernández: 'Tachas,' " *El Zócalo*, January 30, 1958, 3.

[5] Rius Facius, "Efrén Hernández," *Excelsior*, March 2, 1958, 3.

[6] María Luisa Mendoza, "Efrén el grande y el pequeño Hernández," *Excelsior*, March 17, 1957, 2, 4.

[7] See "De la república de los mexicanos," *Presente*, January 12, 1946, 12.

[8] Cortés Tamayo, "Con el lápiz suelto," *El Día*, May 3, 1963, 3. See also "Con el lápiz suelto," *La Prensa Gráfica*, January 12, 1946, 7.

"his voice like a single string of a guitar, tremulous but with intonation." [9] Gonzalo Alfredo Andrade called attention to his clear voice, his small body, which he loved to dress in "shirts of loud colors," his large, very fine hands, which "moved to the rhythm of his voice that seemed to sing"; in short, a man "very small and slender, saturated with nerves, humble in his human greatness." [10]

The man within possessed attributes and qualities not commonly found in the general run of mortals, and a whole crowd of his contemporaries testify to this fact. Dr. Pascual Aceves Barajas, a lifelong friend of the Hernández family, emphasized the "honest and Christian" quality of Hernández's background and described his life as "errant and humble, like that of Pío Baroja." [11] Octavio Bustamente described him as a noisy man of letters who would have accepted with equal humility the profound and abnegating silence of the Franciscans. "Slender, short in stature, serene in his movements, Efrén Hernández longed to be one of that small group of men who go through life making of reality an eternal dream." [12] Antonio Rius Facius wrote that Hernández mixed ingenuousness with the most perspicacious irony, that he accepted life as it was, that the poor man to him was not "an angry anarchist" nor the rich man "a pitiless and degenerate employer, and that he accepted reality and copied it in the difficult simplicity of his "elegant language." [13]

Marco Antonio Millán emphasized Hernández's love and

[9] Poniatowska, "Tachas," *Novedades*, February 2, 1957, 3.
[10] Andrade, "Un intento de concepción de un universo," *Nosotros*, September 3, 1949, 36–37.
[11] Aceves Barajas, "Vida, consagración y ausencia de Efrén Hernández," *El Universal*, March 2, 1958, 1.
[12] Bustamente, "A la carta: Homenaje a Tachas," *El Universal Gráfico*, May 21, 1949, 6.
[13] Rius Facius, "Efrén Hernádez," *Excelsior*, March 2, 1958, 3.

sympathy for his fellow man.[14] He pointed up the inconsistency, in the poet's judgment, anent the spiritual and material inequities of Mexico—the injustices, the social errors. He explained Hernández's idea that the obligatory rural service of the military should be transformed into a "theoretical and practical course in agronomy with an ideological and moral revaluation of all factors pertaining to the countryside, in order to achieve a better common existence." [15] This revised practice, Hernández felt, would do away with the presumptuousness of the army. Further, it would reconcile thousands of men with nature and its pristine values. They would be enriched and tempered by the spirit of the farmer and the disciplines of labor and thus would raise the level of the whole country.

Such personal testimonies are revealing, and their composite, final effect must approach a valid portrait of the man; but it must be remembered that Hernández himself would have played at least a minor role in the formulation of such a mosaic biography. He was concerned with his image, his place in history, the literary currents that did or did not follow his bent, his own theories of literature, and his own philosophical presuppositions. His comments, formal and informal, oral and written, essayistic and fictionalized, are incorporated in the voices of his friends and those he influenced. How could it be otherwise? He obviously wanted to find and to inspire new literary talent, and he came to know young writers through his regular attendance at two clubs sponsored by the Instituto Nacional de Bellas Artes: Martes Poéticos and Viernes Literarios. He also met fre-

[14] See Millán, "El fértil martirio de Efrén Hernández debe ser mejor estimado," *El Libro y el Pueblo*, IV (September 2, 1963), 5.
[15] Millán, "Efrén Hernández: Su inconformidad responsable y esperansada," *Novedades*, January 28, 1962, 3.

quently with youthful groups for coffee-drinking sessions at the Café de Chinos on the Calle del Carmen. It was he who discovered Juan Rulfo, a well-known writer of Mexico today. And it has been claimed that he had a marked influence upon many of the present-day Mexican writers, among them, Dolores Castro, Rosario Castellanos, Emilio Carbellido, Ramón Mendoza Montes, Sergio Magaña, Miguel Guardia, and Luisa Josefina Hernández. If Efrén Hernández, the man, has thus contributed at least indirectly to our view of his personal and social concerns, he has given more, and more directly, to the profile of his literary and philosophical attitudes. One turns primarily, then, to Hernández himself for these testimonies.

In prologues, in newspapers, and in literary magazines are to be found his various philosophical essays, as well as his literary criticism. Hernández made no attempt at a systematic philosophy. He was, however, a deep thinker and a student of many of the various philosophical systems. His approach to philosophical thought was informal and personal, usually light enough to be entertaining to the public and always expressed with an unambiguous *yo.*

In unpublished personal notes,[16] Hernández defined art as magic, as enveloped in the same mystery that envelops life itself. He referred to it as the reality of man, since it contains the two planes that determine man: the conscious, or physical, and the subconscious, or metaphysical. Its very essence, he felt, lay in the affinity between these two planes—an affinity involving the relationship, the accommodation, of the two. He believed that the purpose of art was to project the essence of the individual and to give to man humility by giving him love, satisfaction, and peace. Teresa Bosque Lastra hypothesizes that Hernández may seem to have taken

16 See Bosque Lastra, 103.

this esthetic goal from Unamuno, in the sense that his works are not merely didactic but are dedicated, also, to the search for beauty.[17] The similarity is indeed striking.

According to his own testimony, Hernández dedicated himself to the quest for truth, for the meaning of reality. He struggled to avoid as far as humanly possible all distorted images, all falsity, because, as he explained it:

... la mentira es, en mi concepto, enemiga del hombre y de la literatura del hombre; cierto que en comparación de la inmovilidad y de la esterilidad del pensamiento y de la imaginación, es una mejoría; pero por mucho que se conceda que es, siempre hará papeles tristes, pálidos, y la habilidad para mentir jamás merecerá la gracia de poder llegar a ser paragonada con la capacidad de intuir realidad y valores verdaderos.[18]

In his struggle for truth he tried to learn the answers through reason and intelligence, Pascal's *l'esprit de géométrie*. He felt that the faculty which brings to man his greatest peace and his clearest understanding of himself is intelligence . . . that error and ignorance are the two forms of "la ininteligencia." [19] Xavier Villaurrutia had, however, warned him that one cannot find truth by looking for it; that "all that we can do is to stumble across it at a precise moment." [20] Hernández, who could not accept the orthodox faith which Villaurrutia so easily embraced, had apparently denied to his friend that he could accept the idea of the revelation of truth through inspiration. It is, therefore, paradoxical that in spite of his penchant for reason in both prose and poetry, he espoused most warmly *l'esprit de finesse* and revealed that it was his heart which intuitively gave

[17] *Ibid.*, 89.
[18] *Obras*, 155.
[19] Efrén Hernández, "Algunos pensamientos que surgieron tratando de encontrar una definición de poesía," *El Libro y el Pueblo*, II (July–August, 1941), 11, 16.
[20] Expressed in "El señor de palo," *ibid.*, X (December, 1932), 14.

him what his reason could not, the meanings and collective meaning of love, beauty, and truth.

During an interview with Gonzalo Alfredo Andrade, Hernández defined literature and explained what he felt to be its goal.

Lo que para aparecer necesita el conducto de la inteligencia del hombre (las realizaciones artísticas) es subcreación; por eso, la literatura es una subespecie —creatura de creaturas— y en cuanto al objeto de la literatura, probablemente es aproximar al hombre a la inteligencia.[21]

Then he added that, among the things that are within the reach of our senses, that which is closest to intelligence is "sanctity." Ranked under sanctity came philosophy, and below philosophy, art. The highest art he defined as literature. He believed that true literature must engender philosophy or, at least, laic saints or heroes and that it should be able to convey a "credible illusion." He did not think that Mexican literature had attained a very high point, because it had not carried out these functions; but he added that the time was approaching in present-day literature when existing inquietudes of a "peculiar flavor" would carry it to a more positive level. He called José Vasconcelos a type of creative philosopher. "Mal o bien, él es el único que ha realizado filosofía en alguna medida." Sor Juana and Amado Nervo he named as two Mexican writers who had been able to "make us fall into illusion," and he called José Gorostiza one of the greatest poets of the Spanish language. Alfonso Reyes, on the other hand, he called more a brilliant figure "de academia y de renombre y lucimiento" than an artist.[22]

The illusive and elusive significance of the psyche seems to have haunted the thought of Hernández. He reasoned that it is perhaps the evidence of the potential possession of

---

[21] Andrade, "Un intento de concepción de un universo," 36.
[22] *Ibid.*, 37.

infinity and that, at least to some extent, we can, by deduction, legitimately suspect that "lo definitivo, la plenitud del ser," consists of something very similar to the possession of eternity.[23] Thus in searching for the transcendental meaning of life, he searched within his psychic self—specifically within the experiences of the dream. "Then, out of breath, I came to where I live to search for myself." [24] For him these experiences were the experiences of the world of the soul, the experiences of the Platonic realm of ideas and of memory. Deep within this psychic self there is an area where "everything is a closed wall, single bedrooms; / my inwardness is closed doors." [25] Here, when the eyes close their windows "other eyes open, eyes that do not help you see the world but, rather, help you look within yourself." With these other eyes, one realizes an infinite number of things— "blacker than weariness and night, colder than the cold that sends shivers down the spine, more opaque than dreams." [26] In this secluded and solitary spot, the sensory world disappears and:

> ... ésta es la hora
> desnuda, sin cortejo, seca y sola,
> que no distraen las flores,
> que no turban los pájaros o encantan
> con sus neblinas lentas los crepúsculos ... [27]

It is interesting that Hernández was directly concerned with a distinction between *el dormir* and *el sueño*, a distinction he formulated in an essay.

Por la noche no hay nada que vencer. Silencio, sombra. Los objetos reales —cosas— silenciosos y apagados, áislanse o queda interrumpida toda conexión entre el mundo exterior y la conciencia.

[23] Efrén Hernández, "Algunos pensamientos que surgieron tratando de encontrar una definición de poesía," 11, 16.
[24] *Obras*, 374.   [26] *Ibid.*, 297.
[25] *Ibid.*, 13.   [27] *Ibid.*, 13.

Esto es el dormir.

Mas los objetos psíquicos, en el alma turbada que no logra aquietarse, suelen tomar el campo, entrar en las recámaras de la conciencia, y turbar su reposo.

Es que hay abajo, en el subsuelo psíquico, algún objeto extraño, inconciliable que no puede ser reconocido ni se logra expulsar.

.   .   .   .

¿Quién sabe en qué manera y por qué causas, cosas que no nos atañen, que no llegamos a comprender cómo es que nos atañen, llegan a aposentarse dentro de nosotros, protestan su presencia, y nos atormentan como pecados nuestros? [28]

In spite of his protestations concerning the satisfaction afforded him by reason, Hernández realized reason's great limitations:

> Ay, angustiado polvo,
> ¿cómo has de alimentarnos, vida oscura
> y seca de la tierra,
> cómo te sorberemos, sin raíz,
> si nuestros ojos
> presienten ser azules? [29]

How can the organs of this world—reason and sense—suffice if man has the instinctive desire for faith? With Hernández there were times when faith almost deserted him and reason was on the verge of victory. Under such circumstances he expressed a fear that his soul be lost to him completely:

> Y dentro en la honda caja, do la esencia
> indivisible, ingénita se esconde,
> disuelta o repartida,
> débil, amenazada y sin sosiego,
> huyendo a no escaparse,
> se refugia en sí misma, y concentrándose,
> se va empequeñeciendo, hasta perderse.[30]

---

[28] Efrén Hernández, "Un reportazgo ejemplar," *Futuro*, No. 51 (May, 1940), 50–51.

[29] *Obras*, 29.

[30] *Ibid.*, 30.

Out of his inquietude brought on by reason, he wrote a philosophical essay, "Incógnita es incógnita," in which he summed up his transcendental yearnings:

> Usar la palabra Dios es como usar la letra x.
> A la mayor inteligencia corresponde más asombro, no menos misterio.
> Se cree sabio aquel que enciende una bujía y jamás le da la espalda para que no anochezca; el que jamás ha abierto sus puertas a la noche ni ha arrojado sus senderos a la profundidad.[31]

He was fascinated, as was Pascal, by the fact that, wherever we look—outside, inside, towards the past, towards the future—we are surrounded by "twilight." The word *God* thus posed a particular problem for him. He pointed out that we fill the meaning of this word with concepts, just as if we should take the ashes of a burned heart and to each pinch give a different idea: nostalgia, fear, suffering, hate, thirst, and love. But the designations would be assigned blindly; and who, Hernández questioned, is to say that they are right?

Ali Chumacero wrote in the prologue to Hernández's *Obras* that his mental inquietudes neither led him towards the prophetic nor converted him into a "literato" who, in so many pages, attempted to resolve the persistence of his doubts. "Hizo el consabido viaje alrededor de su cuarto, deslizándose en multiples divagaciones, y allí mismo quemó las naves." Chumacero believed that his excellence lay precisely in this fact, "en que, si bien dilató el juego de los temas, no quiso salir del leve purgatorio de su alma." [32]

Out of this concept of the inconformity of man with himself grew Hernández's idea of the hero. He felt that it was from this absence of convenient accommodation that

---

[31] Efrén Hernández, "Manojo de aventuras (Una página inédita): 'Incógnita es incógnita,'" *Novedades*, January 28, 1962, 3.
[32] *Obras*, viii.

there proceeded the archetypical idealizations of the master, the guide, the wise man, the prophet, and the saint. In a short story, Hernández dramatized a situation wherein a sick man builds castles in the air, imagining himself healthy; and the sicker he is, the healthier he dreams of himself as being.[33] And in an essay he pointed out his belief that mature people generally feel constrained to conduct themselves according to the dreams that some men—those who pass through life always flying low—dream; while immature and youthful people only visualize phantoms of archetypes. He added, however, that, as these latter develop, the phantoms will be done away with and true heroes will take their places.[34]

It was out of this concept, also, that his attitude toward death must have developed. Unlike Unamuno in his agonizing struggle toward *el no morir* ("not dying"), Hernández could face the unknown with hope. He considered the past (memory) as the picture of the future; and he came to feel that life and death, rather than being contrary to each other, were only two modes of the same thing. Hernández held that "of all the institutions of life . . . the most universally categorical and imperative and the only one before which all the others are powerless is that of death." He felt that man naturally struggles toward *el no morir* but that "finally, when life reaches a certain level of development and perfection, man sees himself inexplicably constrained to forget himself in his actions, and this is the very thing that happens when life finally is elevated to the level which marks the appearance of the supreme artist and of the true hero." [35]

In the poem, "Sumarísimo extracto de una definición,"

[33] "El señor de palo" (*Obras*, 311–40) is a perfect example of this premise.
[34] Efrén Hernández, "Manojo de aventuras (Una página inédita): 'Incógnita es incógnita,'" 3.
[35] Efrén Hernández, "Alusiones," *La República*, XV (October 1, 1949), 21.

Hernández explains his idea of the relationship between life and death:

> Lo que una vez, perecedero, ha sido;
> lo que ahora ya no es, lo ahora ausente,
> lo desaparecido,
> la memoria lo guarda
> dolorida, amorosa, insuficiente.

Out of eternity (*el no estar*) man passes into life (*el estar*) and only "insufficient memory" keeps alive in the human mind the connection between the two. "Recordar es arder, morir, quemarse un poco / por reencender un poco lo extinguido." Life is a continuous movement toward death in its struggle to remember.

> Y acabar de morir,
> morir enteramente,
> huir con la memoria,
> con toda la memoria
> y todo el corazón, a donde ha huído
> lo desaparecido
> para siempre jamás; eso es olvido.[36]

El estar finally returns completely to *el no estar*.

In all his works he claimed to have sought for true poetic expression, which he defined as "the eternal expression that arouses emotion and reflects beauty without the necessity of deceptions, of linguistic *malabarismos*, or of intellectual adaptation of the theme." [37] In a short story, "Un clavito en el aire," he expressed an idea of esthetics—simple, precise, difficult to achieve: "Art is like the professional ability of a tailor, whose only virtue should consist of giving to each thought a suitable dress." [38] It may be taken as his own working theory.

[36] *Obras*, 54–55.
[37] Efrén Hernández, "Algunos pensamientos que surgieron tratando de encontrar una definición de poesía," 16.
[38] *Obras*, 341.

Perhaps as revealing as his direct pronouncements regarding what literature ought to do are his reactions to literary movements. He made very clear that in his quest for truth he searched not as an existentialist nor as a surrealist but, as he defined it, as an "esencialista." He impugned Sartre and, concerning existentialist literature, which he called "literatura comprometida," he claimed not to have formed a definite theory. Essence, to Hernández, was eternal; it did not follow existence. Its meaning could be revealed only to the psychic processes of the mind, not to the disjointed processes of the surrealist dream. Thus his *esencialismo* was completely different from existentialism and from surrealism.

Ecce homo poetaque: a mixture, subtle and engrossing at the same time, of spiritual intensities and pragmatic inadequacies, a creature buffeted by his situation yet mindful of the higher nature proffered by his interiority; a man, at the last, heedless of time yet living and writing uniquely and pridefully within his own time.

Chapter II

PHILOSOPHICAL MENTORS

IT WAS IN the great Spanish past of the Siglo de Oro, with its neo-Platonic philosophy, its humanistic desire for knowledge, its respect for form, its balance of form and content, that Hernández found the heart and, to some extent, the manner of artistic expression in both his prose and his poetry. In an interview with María Luisa Mendoza, Hernández said, "I have dedicated myself to the Spanish language poets. Not to the contemporary ones, however; they are not good ones." [1] And it was among the Spanish mystics of the Golden Age, Cervantes, and to a lesser degree, Gracián, that he found his greatest mentors.

Hernández espoused mysticism in its broad sense, a mysticism which did not seek the symbolic union with God, as did that of Santa Teresa de Jesús and San Juan de la Cruz, but a mysticism that in its feeling for the absolute, opposed the positions of naturalism and rationalism. It led him to lonely contemplation and to lyricism. Within his solitude—within the dwelling place of his soul—he searched for himself and for truth. In this *recámara* there was a door, an exit to the sensory world, and there was a window, an opening through which one might look toward the things of this

---

[1] María Luisa Mendoza, "Efrén el grande y el pequeño Hernández," 2.

world, beyond that, toward the heavens, and still far beyond that, toward truth. But even in this inner room, because of the dust (doubt), he was disoriented. His "anhelo," (the yearning within him) spoke to him:

> ... ya es tan noche;
> durmiéronse mis pies, andar no acierto,
> no puedo andar, amor; se han cerrado
> mis fuerzas, y mis ojos,
> de la palabra abrirse no están ciertos;
> ya alumbrarnos no saben; busca a tientas,
> tal vez, estoy aquí, pero, quién sabe,
> tal vez, estoy más lejos ...
> ... en realidad no sé,
> se me extravió el nivel del horizonte,
> la parte en que es la puerta, los senderos
> por do se va del lecho a la ventana ... [2]

There was such a close affinity between the thought of Hernández and that of Fray Luis de León that the Augustinian was possibly his most distinct philosophical mentor. Indeed, he furnished both the base for Hernández's philosophical concept of the Platonic doctrines of ideas and of memory and an approach wherein sentiment was superimposed upon intellectual ideas concerning God, nature, and man. Perhaps the most obvious similarity in the thought of the two men is one of controlling mood or tone. Both felt themselves somehow isolated or imprisoned, with the result that both felt a peculiar nostalgia for that ideal world out of reach. In "A Felipe Ruiz," Fray Luis wrote:

> ¿Quándo será que pueda
> libre de esta prisión volar al cielo,
> Felipe, y en la rueda
> que huye más del suelo,
> contemplar la verdad pura sin duelo? [3]

---

[2] *Obras*, 34.
[3] Fray Luis de León, *Poesías completas*, Vol. I, 2nd ed. (Buenos Aires: Editorial Sopena Argentina, 1942), p. 19.

In these lines, Hernández described a correspondent remoteness:

> Al pez fuera del agua, separado
> del elemento suyo,
> de su océano amado, y por remota,
> desconocida mano transladado
> a donde ni una gota
> existe del precioso
> líquido deseado,
> mi espectro lastimoso
> comparo ... [4]

The concepts of ideas and memory, of idealism itself, of the harmony of the universe, and of the duality of the body and the soul—ideas which had been enunciated by Plato and based upon the writings of Pythagoras and Parmenides—are keystones in the thought of Fray Luis. For example, in the poem to Salinas, Fray Luis wrote of memory:

> A cuyo son divino
> el alma, que en olvido está sumida,
> tornó a cobrar el tino
> y memoria perdida
> de su origen primera esclarecida.[5]

The whole of Hernández's poetic expression is permeated with this idea. For him memory is the connecting thread which unites and gives meaning to a coexistence of the soul and eternity.

> Tu causa fue el desprecio
> original; la falta,
> la inconexión, la ausencia,
> en sí mismos dolidos ... Todo ausencias,
> preterición, distancia, mármol, hielo,
> separación y daño.

[4] *Obras*, 30.
[5] Luis de León, 10.

Tu parte fue la noche,
tu origen las orillas,
tu antecedente, tú lejos de ti
—yo aún sin esperanza, lejos, lejos—
y tu nido el abismo.

Te instituyó el principio
de aspiración, que ordena
que se llene el vacío,
que impere la presencia, y la presencia
entre dentro en sí misma y se acompañe.

Y bajo la apariencia
de forestal criatura, tul volátil,
oasis trashumante,
peregrino palmar, acomodado
a la viudez del viento, tú, pasando,
con vuelo sin cuidado,
nuestra insondable alianza rubricaste. ...[6]

He dedicated a long poem, "Recogido en la cuenca," to memory.

In his desire for peace and solitude, Hernández turned, as had Fray Luis, to the poetic inspiration of Horace. In a newspaper essay he expressed a strong admiration for the Latin poet and added that in this world of today, with its great intellectual and moral responsibilities, we should turn again to the poetry of Horace and "respirarla con fuerza." [7]

In extolling the virtues of the contemplative life, Fray Luis chose the "Beatus ille" of Horace as the model for his poem, "La vida retirada." Expressing the same sentiment, Hernández not only chose these two poetic expressions as his models; he gave to his poem the same name as that of Horace's poem, and he began his "Beatus ille" with the opening lines of "La vida retirada": "Qué descansada vida /

[6] *Obras*, 47.
[7] See Efrén Hernández, "Evocación de Horacio: Poema de Salomón de la Selva," *La República*, October 15, 1949, 20.

la del que huye el mundanal ruido. ..." [8] In the description
of the joys of country life many of the same symbols, metaphors, and descriptions of the sensory world are to be found
in "La vida retirada" and in Hernández's "Beatus ille." The
tone is similar in both poems. The conclusions, however, are
somewhat different. In "La vida retirada," Fray Luis yearned
for peace:

> Y mientras miserable-
> mente se están los otros abrasando
> con sed insaciable
> del peligroso mundo,
> tendido yo a la sombra esté cantando ... [9]

Hernández, in keeping with his notion of the true hero,
turns his poem from the discovery of peace to a return to
the "guerra":

> ... en subida
> región, y contemplando,
> a un lado la escondida
> senda, y al otro la ciudad henchida.
>
> Y con novel postura,
> ya al bien tras que venía, ora se cierra,
> y abierto a la ternura
> que ahermana cielo y tierra,
> cogida al fin la paz, vuelve a la guerra.[10]

Like Fray Luis, Hernández embraced the ethics of Seneca.
He identified virtue with wisdom, and he believed in the
necessity for overcoming self. "Era preciso," he wrote, "que
se aviniera a sufrir con estoicismo y humildad, durante el
tiempo que fuera preciso, todo lo que se presentara." [11] His
belief, however, did not lead him to that passive life partially
implied by Stoic tranquility. Fray Luis found tranquility
through the firm religious beliefs which Hernández could

[8] *Obras*, 59.
[9] Luis de León, 9.

[11] *Ibid.*, 194.
[10] *Obras*, 63.

not embrace. In "Exposición del libro de Job," Fray Luis treated the subject of suffering and came to the conclusion that the things of this world are vanity and that the good life must be, like Job's, one of suffering. He saw also that only through suffering can temporal life lead to ultimate truth. Hernández, too, was evidently influenced by the sufferings of Job. Preceding the first poem in his book, *Entre apagados muros*, is the following quotation:

> Mide mi corazón la noche.
> Libro de Job

For Hernández, whose life was one of much pain and whose writings dwell often on the topic of suffering, stoicism was always a positive attitude that opened a way to perception of truth. Job displayed the real condition of man. As with Luis, Hernández came to see that everything of the world was vanity[12] and that death was the mocking end of much that was falsely imagined to have ultimate value.

In the works of both men are to be found expressions of the conventional idea that life is a dream. In "La vida retirada," Fray Luis pictured life as a broken dream, and there are allusions to this concept in Hernández's works. In one of his philosophical essays he stated "y en éste todo, todo este vivir y ser y mundo, acaso todo es sueño, pues todo parece sueño y todo tiene y deja sabor a vanidad, nonada, y sueño."[13]

Given a common nostalgia for the ideal realm, a similar emphasis on the semidivine function of Memory, a common ethical and esthetic *summum bonum*, generally the same attitude toward human suffering, and common motifs, it is hardly surprising that Fray Luis and Efrén Hernández should display a similar tragic concern for the passing of

---

[12] *Ibid.*, 28.
[13] Efrén Hernández, "Manojo de aventuras (Una página inédita)," 3.

time. To Fray Luis man is cheated by time as well as by the dream:

> El hombre está entregado
> al sueño, de su suerte no cuidando,
> y con paso callado
> el cielo vueltas dando
> las horas del vivir le va hurtando.[14]

Throughout both his poetry and his prose, Hernández likewise demonstrated his unhappiness at the idea of the passage of time. He addressed himself to *el desterrado*, the one taken out of the eternal world of memory:

> A ti, porque saliste
> del recinto sin cinto,
> del corazón sin centro,
> del centro sin orillas.
>
> Y a la luz caminate de los días, ...
>
> A ti, porque sin ancla ni asidero,
> ya eres de nuevo aguja,
> y ves, con inquietud, tu leve sombra,
> sin remedio rodar, del meridiano,
> sobre los cruentos números.[15]

Man must suffer the sad fate of time until the day:

> Cuando el tiempo, su frente de cansancio,
> sus alas doloridas
> y sus pies sin reposo,
> vuelva, al fin, a la casa de sus padres.
>
> Y en el rincón secreto,
> ¡más interno!
> al lecho más profundo
> se entregue, y ya ni él mismo
> atestigüe el silencio
> del recatado soplo con que apague
> y devuelva al misterio un universo.[16]

[14] Luis de León, 16.   [15] *Obras*, 11.   [16] *Ibid.*, 53.

Such a concept of time is admittedly mystical, and indeed the whole of the work of the two men is pervaded by overtones of mysticism. With the appearance of neo-Platonism, shortly before the beginning of the Christian Era, such overtones had begun to creep into the philosophy. In the third century A.D., Plotinus, turning away from the essentially intellectual position of Plato, had set forth his doctrine concerning the union of the soul with God by means of ecstasy as well as by contemplation—a doctrine that was one of the sources of European mysticism. Although the position of Fray Luis, like that of Hernández, was essentially intellectual, both men yearned to feel intuitively the wisdom which human understanding could not reach. Thus in his intimate reaction to the universal unknown, Hernández found responsive notes, also, in the works of Santa Teresa and of San Juan.

The autobiographical character, the use of diminutives, and traces of humor are traits common to the prose works of both Hernández and Santa Teresa. The latter's concept of the dwelling place of the soul—of God—demonstrates certain similarities to that of Hernández. She wrote of the *moradas*, the dwelling places of the soul, one within the other, and in the center the home or palace of the King; and the whole she visualized as being alive with light. It is this inward center, this dwelling place of the soul, which Hernández described in these words:

> Hondo, incomunicado,
> entre apagados muros,
> hay un recinto hermético, cerrado, fidelísimo,
> de libertad y paz,
> en realidad y luz, siempre encendido.
>
> (Eres como una esfera
> vertiginosamente conturbada;
> giras todo, te cambias,

vives en la tormenta, entre zozobras
y continuos naufragios,
centrífugas corrientes
te apartan largamente de tu centro;
pero en tu centro duras,
tienes un eje fijo en que no cambias.) [17]

Spanish mysticism was, of course, only a manifestation of mysticism in general, which, in the strict sense of the word, entails five steps: *conversión, vía purgativa, vía iluminativa, noche oscura,* and *vía unitiva.* The first four steps had been defined by Plato; then Plotinus and other early Christian mystics had added the fifth stage, that of ecstasy, of spiritual union. The intellectual road ended with the fourth stage. Thus while the way of mysticism led Santa Teresa and San Juan to the symbolic union with God, this way was closed to Hernández. For him,

> ... de esta región no pueden
> recibirse mensajes ...
> de ella no cogemos
> sino hálitos más vagos,
> aún, que presentimientos.[18]

The outstanding images in the work of San Juan are distance and darkness, a spiritualized night in which the sensory world is erased and the only light comes from the glowing heart as it struggles towards the mystical union with God. In the work of Hernández the heart, the soul, is more often wandering in the dark night, "a blind abyss, lost in the emptiness of itself." [19] He could not, like Santa Teresa and San Juan, reach the mystical union: "Subiendo la escalera grada a grada / vino que ya cerraste tu recámara." [20] When, however, the soul does seem to catch a glimpse of hope and revelation, his symbol is light, which is also the great symbol of Plato and of Fray Luis.

---

[17] *Ibid.,* 31. [18] *Ibid.,* 32. [19] *Ibid.,* 27. [20] *Ibid.,* 14.

De tiempo en tiempo largo en breve espacio,
el alma, levemente
surge a una escasa luz ... [21]

Both in his philosophy and in his style, Hernández exhibited marked similarities to baroque writers of seventeenth-century Spain. The social and political conditions of his country may have contributed to the anxieties that one assumes to accompany or cause such a style of thought, but it was the conflict between the realm of God and the realm of man—that conflict so typically baroque—which seems to have been at the base of Hernández's disquietude. In his manner of writing this tension is revealed. More than once in his poetry he used the phrase, "mi voluta"; and *voluta* is the name of the curved line used in the highly ornamental Ionic capital.

His style is often obscure, which tends to limit the appeal of his works to the cultured minority. Such exclusiveness is certainly *culteranismo*; however, in his use of allegory, play on words, hyperbaton, antithesis, and wit, there are the marks of *conceptismo*. As did those writers of the baroque age, he took from abroad—in his case, Spain—what he deemed good and elevated, and to it he added popular elements. His style is in many ways reminiscent of Gracián, but here similarities serve mainly to point up contrasts. Gracián's suspicious and negative attitude toward life agreed with the pessimism of the *pícaro* of the seventeenth century. Although Hernández could never have accepted such a pessimistic view, he did agree with Gracián that man is in a constant struggle with life. Both men were didactic in their approach to literature, and sharp traces of humor and psychological penetration are common to the work of each.

Like the hero of Gracián, the protagonist of Hernández

[21] *Ibid.*, 33.

is neither a sword brandisher nor a superman. Gracián disagreed with the bitter determinism of the *pícaro* concerning the end of life. While this rogue was indifferent towards the idea of immortality, Gracián believed that it might be won by the life of successful struggle—through will. Gracián's hero is thus a man of intellect and understanding, judgment and individuality, one who can win fame in the world of action. The Christian ideal of love was never far enough away from the mind and heart of Hernández for him to have firmly held such a premise. Thus Gracián's man of prudence could have held little appeal for Hernández. In the broad view of life presented in Gracián's allegory, *El Criticón*, there is a severe indictment of human folly, and the only possible hero is the man of discretion. Hernández had many protagonists, but the true hero mixes heart with intellect, and his aim is not to win fame but, rather, to win peace between his rationality and his intuition.

The works of Hernández display a vacillation in the will of the narrator or writer. Generally, there is the will to persevere, to struggle to achieve some goal; at times, however, the will seems almost overcome, almost impotent. In truth, this lack of will represents not a negative quality—not the almost fatalistic determinism of the rogue—rather, it is a positive overcoming of the will. The attitude grew out of the attraction which the doctrine of quietism held for Hernández. Its influence at times seems to have led him to the effort to overcome the more positive concept of the function of the will. It was Miguel de Molinos, a heterodox mystic and the only great Spanish mystic of the seventeenth century, who most especially propounded this doctrine, which carried mysticism to its extreme limits in recommending an absolute quietude of the soul, the killing of all desire. A century earlier, San Juan had arrived at the line of demarcation between orthodoxy and heterodox quietism. San Juan, however, because of his sincere acceptance of the doctrines of the church, never stepped over the boundary.

Molinos scorned the active life, the will, or *voluntad*, which had seemed so important to most of the sixteenth-century mystics. He sought pure contemplation, and the last chapter of his *Guía espiritual* has the air of a prayer in praise of Nirvana. This passive state, the church charged, would carry one to a spiritual nothingness. Although the doctrine was prohibited by the Inquisition, it held great appeal for many people, and its influence was especially strong in France, where it inspired Fénelon, whose *Explication des Maximes des saints* was condemned by the pope.

Quietism seems sometimes with Hernández to be the only solution. He held that each human life could be a river bed through which flowed a stream of anguish. The anguish flooding the life of Nicomaco, the protagonist of the short novel, *Cerrazón sobre Nicomaco: Ficción harto doliente*—an anguish which in this case is the result of jealousy—finally forces this self-centered man towards the philosophical position of quietism. As a patient in a hospital, during his waking hours he is under the care of others; he is without words, without thoughts, without desires. In the story, "El señor de palo," Hernández likewise showed interest in quietism as a sort of solution. At the very first of the story, the paralytic, Domingo, gives an intimation of quietism in speaking of motorcycle wheels on his wheelchair:

Y las ruedas de mi sillón de paralítico son de motocicleta. Este detalle complica inverosímilmente mis ideas. Hace tiempo, conocí a una muchacha que se prostituyó. A medida que se degeneraba, se abatía su ánimo, hasta llegar su abatimiento a convertirla en una paralítica del alma.[22]

At the end of the story, Domingo's desire for life is dead. His feelings are more nearly in keeping with the true state

[22] *Ibid.*, 311.

of quietism. Remembering that "está prohibido trasgredir la Constitución, inviolable de por sí, de la muerte, cuyo artículo uno, que es el fundamental, estatuye el silencio," he observes:

Y yo, dócil y dulcemente, amoroso de mi perfección, me he callado y en este capítulo no hablo ya. Venga el músico más privilegiado del mundo, el gran músico que tenga el más fino de todos los oídos del mundo, y coloque el oído en la losa de mi gaveta, y oiga.

"Son tres las gradaciones del silencio," nos enseña Miguel de Molinos: Silencio de palabras, más hondo, silencio de pensamientos, infinitamente hondo, silencio de deseos.

El músico, si ha oído bien, os diga: En este capítulo Domingo ya no habla. En este capítulo Domingo ya no piensa. En este capítulo Domingo ya no sufre. Es decir, Domingo ya no quiere, no desea; se ha hundido en el silencio, y ahora ya es paralítico hasta del corazón.[23]

Schopenhauer regarded tragedy as the summit of poetic art, because he felt tragedy to be an essential part of life; and the only way in which man may overcome himself in this life, he felt, is through suffering. Not only did Nietzsche attempt to repudiate such a theory, he disagreed emphatically with Schopenhauer's definition of pessimistic art (tragedy) and with the latter's belief that tragedy teaches resignation. To Nietzsche, life was a tragic process, but tragedy was a source of regeneration. It was Nietzsche's theory of tragedy upon which Hernández may have based his concept of the drama.

Various twentieth-century critics have identified Nietzsche with Gracián, one of these being Azorín, who "intuitively" made his identification and who, according to Villaurrutia, was a mentor to Hernández.[24] At times in the works of Hernández there are the same resignation, the same melancholy, the same stoicism shown by Azorín. Both favored

[23] *Ibid.*, 340.   [24] See Villaurrutia, 15.

an impressionistic style, in which the presentation of the effects of a scene and the emotions of the characters are emphasized, with little or no importance being placed on concrete detail. Both concentrated on inconsequential events, the miniature, believing that the enduring realities of life are to be found in *las pequeñas cosas* rather than in history and great events, which pass away.

An anonymous writer elaborates further upon the relationship of Hernández and Azorín. Hernández's themes, he says, are often almost unimportant, just as are the themes of the early works of Azorín. With Hernández they are often merely a pretext for "very delicate soliloquy, in which appear flashes of sharp malice alternating with penumbrae of enchanting innocence." [25] In the works of the two there is nothing solemn, majestic, nor high-sounding, nothing of the heroic or of the simply ironic. Azorín's placid style was an ideal vehicle for expressing the hermetic and intimate qualities of his private world. At times this was also true of Hernández. More often, however, Hernández, contrary in essence to Azorín, superimposed his feelings over his style, ignored any feeling of gentleness, and escaped from simplicity to irony—an irony at times bitter; at others, disillusioned.

These, then, seem to be the chief philosophical mentors of Efrén Hernández: Fray Luis de León; Santa Teresa de Jesús; San Juan de la Cruz; Gracián; Miguel de Molinos; and, at least second-hand through Azorín, Nietzsche. There remains, however, one figure whose inspiration must be called predominant in the shaping of the intellectual attitudes and emotional virtualities of Hernández. This figure looms so large in the history of Spanish literature that all writers after him have had to react, either positively or negatively, to the force of his ideas and his prose. Hernández did more than react. He had a direct affinity for Cervantes.

[25] "Efrén Hernández: Cuentos," *Letras de México*, July 14, 1941, 15.

Chapter III

DUALISM IN THE PROSE FICTION: THE CERVANTINE QUALITY

THE INFLUENCE OF Cervantes on the thought and artistic expression of Hernández is most obvious in the novel, *La paloma, el sótano y la torre.* Here is presented a psychological study of the quarrel between the head and the heart, between the relative and the absolute, between the real and the ideal, in the quest for the successful life. Its premise and philosophical conclusion are that only in illusion can mankind find the way to the successful life through "el sutil ingenio ... el infecundo y fraccionario *pensar el bien*"; that the only true way lies in the "sustancioso e integral *vivir el bien* ... la iluminada, auténtica, profunda, verdadera inteligencia." [1]

Much of the action as well as much of the philosophical rhetoric in the novel takes place in the dream. This circumstance points to the traditional and, for Hernández, vital notion that life may be a dream. One of Hernández's friends, José Tiquet, described him as a man to whom reality was an eternal dream.[2] And certainly Hernández would have been in accord with Miguel de Unamuno, who held, with Segismundo, that even in dreams nothing can be lost by "el

[1] *Obras,* 89.

[2] José Tiquet, "Efrén Hernández: El hombre y su obra," *Novedades,* January 28, 1962, 1.

33

hacer bien," since all generous actions transcend the dream of life.[3]

While the plot of this work—a short poetic novel divided into six parts, or chapters—bears little resemblance to that of Cervantes's masterpiece, there are many analogies to be drawn between the two. Joaquín Casalduero defines the world of the second part of the *Quijote* as political and social, a realm of practical reason, where free will holds sway and man is obliged to decide his own destiny. This *entre claro* state is different from the black and white domain, the world of the real and the ideal in the first part, because here a third element, "Reason, a cloud of dust," intervenes.[4] Here disillusionment leads Don Quijote toward sanity through a typically human psychological process, while, through a similar means, Sancho Panza moves toward more noble desires.[5] It is the second part of the *Quijote*, the world of free will with reason to govern it, which is the philosophical setting for Hernández's novel.

In this arena there is neither an easy way nor any fatalistic destiny. Man has liberty to make his own choices. But liberty is shown capable of degenerating into license, and man's destiny is seen to rest squarely upon himself. "Every grief is the result of a sin, of an error, or an aberration, of ignorance," wrote Hernández. "The years have clearly taught me this, and the voice of the years is the voice of God; every grief, without exception." [6] For the person who has not found himself secure in a state of freedom, who has not made peace between his head and his heart, tears and then, per-

[3] Miguel de Unamuno, *Vida de don Quijote y Sancho, según Miguel de Cervantes Saavedra*, 8th ed. (Buenos Aires: Espasa-Calpe, 1949), 256.

[4] Joaquín Casalduero, *Sentido y forma del Quijote (1605–1615)* (Madrid: Arges, 1949), 210, 243.

[5] See José García López, *Historia de la literatura española*, 7th ed. (Barcelona: Editorial Vicens-Vives, 1962), 260–61.

[6] *Obras*, 120.

haps, the dream are his only consolation. In describing the comfort that tears afford to the heart of man, Hernández uses as a poetic simile the heart of the rose and the dawn:

Dentro del corazón sombrío de la gran rosa colgada, desplegada, apagada, letal y atormentada de la noche, como por causa de su propia apretura y de la de su gran tristeza, en la entraña recóndita surgieron, condensándose, unas gotas. Estas luego rodaron hacia afuera, duraron un momento suspendidas al borde de los pétalos, y al fin se desprendieron como lágrimas. La rosa sintióse como lavada, como suelta, como aliviada y libre de su íntima opresión, abrió con movimientos de párpados sus hojas y el consuelo fue en ellas, no se podría aclarar si semejante, simultáneo, o ya la misma esencia engendradora de la primera luz.[7]

In the novel, Catito, *el sótano* ("the basement") and Fulán, *la torre* ("the tower") are but the two opposing sides of the nature of Efrén Hernández, just as Sancho, a Renaissance man, and Don Quijote, a Gothic man of feeling, represent a baroque complexity of man. Considered alone, each one seems to represent only half of a human being. Catito, the hypocrite, filled with malice and so skinny that his nickname is "el Popote" ("Broomstraw"), puts his complete faith in "ágil, fina, sagaz, escurridiza" intelligence, while his heart lies "pesado, gordo, cegato, obtuso. ..." Throughout most of the story this *pícaro* is worried not at all by his evil acts. It is only a fear of discovery that bothers him. Fulán, on the other hand, is a dreamer, a visionary, who is overcome by "las flamas de vida y ardimiento que arrastran a los hombres a tomar por verdadero lo que los alucina"; he is a man whose nature craves ecstasy. Deep within him, however, there is also "el psíquico complejo en donde tiene origen la facultad azul de la razón." And he examines everything in the light of reason. This is a visible facet of the analogy between Fulán and Don Quijote; for in part 2 of Cervantes's

[7] *Ibid.*, 119.

novel, the knight errant, moving gradually from illusion towards disillusionment, demonstrates a change in his manner of reasoning, away from the inductive towards the deductive, "y ahora digo que es menester tocar las apariencias con la mano para dar lugar al desengaño." [8]

In the eternal battle between his reason and his sentiment, Fulán is blown like a feather in the wind. Because he intuits a lack of some quality that would make him more fully human, a lethal mist gradually develops over the lively flame which has always been such a joyful companion of his senses. Now thinking becomes imperative, even though to him it is an "inherent burden, a stigma, a cross." He realizes, however, that there are areas which reason cannot reach. Each object possesses its own properties, which "surround it, control it, reduce it, and open it to its destiny." But what is the source of these properties? Whence does the governing law emanate? "Is it that in the beginning was the *Código*, only to be followed by chaos, passion, this restless search, this insatiable thirst?" In his longing for peace, like Faust he yearns for more light; like Bergson, for more understanding; like Unamuno, for more warmth.

Juana Andrea Palomino is *la paloma* of the story. She must choose between the *sótano* and the *torre*. Just as the earth awakens to new life with the rising of the sun and the changing of the season, so does the young woman grow away from the sadness and hopelessness brought on by the loss of all that she has held dear—her mother, her father, and her home. "Y esta tierra era ... la propia Juana Andrea revelándose, extendiéndose, la mujer reprimida, sofocada y no reconocida, restituyéndose a su funcional naturaleza, por medio del ensueño." She is the Dulcinea of this story, and

---

[8] Miguel de Cervantes Saavedra, *El ingenioso hidalgo don Quijote de la Mancha*, 8th ed., "Castilian Classics" (Madrid: Espasa-Calpe, 1964), VII, 297.

her tendency is naturally towards the tower. Catito tries to "enchant" Juana Andrea and to bring her down to his level, just as Sancho "enchanted" Dulcinea. Even though she is tempted once or twice to yield, she never reaches the point of accepting the implications of the profane way.

Although the relationship between this psychological novel and *El Quijote* is never openly acknowledged, the author doubtless was aware, and more than aware, of Cervantes's precedent, for Hernández proffers the identical pattern of *El Quijote*. Giants for Don Quijote are windmills for Sancho. And in their search for truth, *la pura esencia*, the knight and his squire constantly encounter difficulty in identifying reality and appearance. So it is, too, with the protagonists of *La paloma, el sótano y la torre*. Specific similarities are, of course, even more telling. In *El Quijote* there is the story within the story, "Maese Pedro"; in Hernández's novel there is the dream within the dream. Just as Cervantes incorporated within his story such popular genres as the sentimental tale, the pastoral, the Moorish, the picaresque, so too did Hernández include in his the romantic, the *costumbrista*, the picaresque, the naturalistic, the realistic, and the historical. Catito, in speaking of "mi tío el borrachito," says that his uncle is on his way to pay a visit to "su dulcinea." Hernández wrote that, when visionary people—like Fulán and Don Quijote—are searching for incorporeal visions in the sky, their feet often stumble; that some have been known to fall down even when the surface is completely smooth; "y no ha faltado el que vuelve en sí ya en el fondo de un pozo." And it is natural that the reader should wonder if Hernández might have intended this as a veiled reference to Sancho and his involuntary fall into the *sima* ("the hole"). Thus not only in longer sentiment but also in the details of narration do the novels *El Quijote* and *La paloma* correspond to each other. This fact granted, or at least posited, the old masterpiece offers invaluable aid in understanding the meaning of Hernández's novel in particular and the subtleties of Hernández's thought in general.

The probing mind of Hernández was greatly preoccupied by the mysterious attributes of time, physical and metaphysical.

Todos ... recuerdos, pensamientos y reconsideraciones surgieron ... y transcurriendo con independencia de este tiempo exterior, sensible cronométrico, rígido, se desenvolvieron dentro de ese otro que no puede medirse y que difiere del primero, principalmente, en que posee una infinita elasticidad.

Suele suceder así: que nos dormimos y soñamos cosas y acontecimientos con duración de un año, y sin embargo, en el reloj la manecilla ha avanzado tan sólo dos minutos.[9]

Surely this is reminiscent of Don Quijote's stay in the Cave of Montesinos. The minute hand had advanced little more than an hour, but the mad knight of la Mancha figured he had spent three days there, dreaming the reason of life. In confronting the conflicting standards of time, the author marshalls once again the two players of his psychological and philosophical game—the man of dreams and the man of social reality.

The route of the illusioned Don Quijote, as he wandered through his native rural countryside, was oddly filled with people. Fulán specifically chose the solitary way and yet wandered in his dream through the city—the city of his heart. "La línea imaginaria en la mitad de la calle imaginaria, era su vía." On the one side was reason; on the other, sentiment. He looked at the grass and at the gorgeous flowers and longed to shut them up in a garden that was his very own. Then little by little he began to "retraerse, a concentrarse ... a introsubjetivizarse", and he realized that

... desde que entrara en el pueblo, ni en las calles, ni en las casas,

9 *Obras*, 151-52.

ni en las tiendas, ni en los talleres, ni en las oficinas, había visto alma viviente. Una quintaesenciada y concentradísima gota de algo más amargo y hondo que cuanto hasta entonces había sentido y conocido, le golpeó con titánica fuerza, como una punta dura como de acero, y fría como de nieve y de vacío, exactamente la mitad del corazón, la mitad de la memoria y el centro de los huesos. Y entendió que no había bajado a ciudad alguna, sino que había andado recorriendo su propio corazón.[10]

While Don Quijote had traveled from adventure to adventure, Fulán, in this city, traveled from empty bench to empty bench; and both went from anguish to desolation to disillusionment.

Hernández felt his thoughts and thought his feelings. When, as Fulán, in his wanderings through the city of his heart, he concentrated upon the mundane things around him—the benches, the number of stones in the pathway—he was, as was almost the case with Sartre's Roquentin, describing mental turmoil in terms of sensory objects. In his interior wanderings, Fulán penetrated deeper and deeper within himself until he finally reached an ideal or metaphysical plane where wind, time, and space seemed to merge; and he seemed to have a passing sight of eternity. "Se le iba el cielo, las llanuras huían hasta perderse, el viento tendía a tiempo, el tiempo a espacio, y el espacio a hambre, a abismal boca abierta." Suddenly understanding flowed over his heart. Until now he and "any slight object" of beauty around him had sufficed; but now he knew that he had been the "victim of hallucinations, of flattery, and of betrayal; that everything was lacking, that nothing fulfilled his deepest needs." Until now he had believed that only physical force had significance, but with new understanding he knew that beyond this force "there is a breath of magic, a miraculous exhalation, a puff of mystery." Until

[10] *Ibid.*, 167–68.

now he had believed that his heart was full; but, in truth, it had been filled only with phantoms. "He had been the victim of a fraud, of a mirage." He discovered that, by having tried to sustain the flame of life through a concentration on things, he had used up his life and let it be consumed. The lamp having run out of oil, the wick was becoming charred. Now he recognized and understood the source of his sadness. "The city of his heart, he had just realized, was full, full of trees, of houses, of streets, of flowers, and of clouds; but also it was empty; and what is a city without people?" [11]

In the midst of such discovery, there came the sudden barking of a dog, and he felt a "little blow" of surprise, a moment of inquietude and shock. It was that "his spirit, going ahead of his body, had not completely detached itself, as it does with death." Rather, it had remained connected as if by a subtle elastic thread; and, at the sudden barking, the spirit had returned to his body as if it had been a button attached to the end of a stretched piece of elastic which had been turned loose. Immediately he recovered his "eyes." Now the *claro oscuro* world had disappeared. Gone, too, was the polarity. He found himself surrounded by a spiritualized landscape, which he saw with more than his human eyes. And there in the obscurity was an unknown young woman, dipping water from the little lake.

In the scant two seconds necessary for her to dip up a bucket of water, "the reflections of the water in the lake had changed N times two hundred times." Led astray by these distorted reflections, or perhaps by those of the moon, he fell into another illusion, and he awoke in some undetermined realm beyond this one. Wherever it was, "the bird of glory sang to him." The unknown woman looked at him, and he approached and addressed her as "Hermana," a mysterious name that, in its context of magic and dream, is strongly reminiscent of Harry Haller's guide and teacher,

[11] *Ibid.*, 169.

Hermine, in Hermann Hesse's *Steppenwolf*. She is, also, a Beatrice figure.

Between them there was a "tonic silence that was neither nothingness nor death nor the silence of death" but, rather, the silence resulting from perfect harmony. Then she, with a smile, rose from the ground and with "direct levitation" came to rest on the bridge. He too, went up to the bridge; and sitting there beside her, the bridge became for him the bench "no solitario" for which he was searching. As she departed from him he came to himself somewhat, and he watched her with his eyes and imagination. Simply because she had passed his way, he felt himself "filled with imponderable expressions without number," and he received an ineradicable mark "que se le esteriotipó." Now he was overcome with the desire to go beyond his body—beyond the place which he occupied in space. During that afternoon he had tried to throw his thought up to the limits of the sky, but the task had been impossible. Following the meeting with the woman—this Beatrice, Dulcinea, and Hermine—he had become a "fountain of gratitude," and now this feeling of thankfulness touched the sky and carried him where thought could not reach. The sky no longer seemed very far away. He reached it with great ease, and his heart was at peace and overflowing with clear understanding and with the universal imperative—at once *caritas* and the Kantian surety of objectively valid morality. Now he might have said with Don Quijote: "I now have free and clear judgment . . . In the nests of yesteryear there are no birds today . . . I was crazy and now I am sane . . ." [12] Now he

---

[12] Cervantes, VIII, 322–28. It is interesting to note that, in the short story, "El señor de palo," Hernández describes the *sueño* ("fancy, imagination") in terms of "pájaros de la cabeza": "Los pájaros de la cabeza que tanto ayudan a desgravitar la vida, los pájaros en que se convierte nuestro fósforo más forforescente, aquel de nuestro fósforo, que, para convertirse en volúmenes de filosofía o de ciencia, o en niños aun rubios, resulta demasiado luminoso" (*Obras*, 331).

knew that for the successful life the two worlds of the human being—the internal and the external, the ideal and the real—can and must exist together. "No longer was it necessary for the day to lose the sun to find its stars . . . thus Fulán saw and lived what he was dreaming and he was fully himself . . ." [13] Fulán, who had been a visionary, now recognized that "the state of faithful, practical lucidity" must exist within the state of ecstasy if either state is to have real meaning; that it is necessary for man to learn to suffer with stoicism and humility; that within the individual there is a mysterious and magic quality that permits man to accommodate himself to this world and to find peace, leaving to the world to come the discovery of perfect truth.

When, some years later, Fulán again met Juana Andrea, he did not recognize her, yet he felt that he had discovered his destiny. To him this meeting was like a remembering—a return of a part of Memory, the eternal, transcendental substance. The picture of Juana Andrea which he had painted in his memory was "an abstraction, an idealization." Just as Dulcinea had represented to Don Quijote the unattainable ideal as well as the way towards that goal, so did Juana Andrea come to represent both to Fulán. The first encounter had made upon his soul such a deep impression that its effects "conditioned his sensibility, placed an enduring stamp upon him, determined the ideal image which he must follow." Thus this very real girl was for him the embodiment of his ideal, and he knew that he had found his "Dulcinea."

Just as practical Sancho had finally fallen into the deep and slippery hole which, according to Casalduero, represented the "entrar en sí," so did pragmatic Catito finally sink into the dream and experience autorevelation. In spite of himself he had gradually come to see Fulán, his rival for the affection

---

[13] *Obras*, 177.

of Juana Andrea, as his ideal person, one whose soul was of "crystalline running waters." Even before Fulán ceased to be the visionary, Catito had come to accept him as his ideal: "De hecho, sin alcanzar a percibirlo, [yo] lo admiraba, lo envidiaba y aún empezaba a hacer por dentro mis pininos de sentirme sentimental y triste, sin ninguna esperanza y sin ningún consuelo. Pantomimas de mi imaginación." [14]

In his illusion, Catito believed that the marriage of Fulán and Juana Andrea had already taken place; and, because of his anguish, he sank deeper and deeper into his own dream. Finally there began to appear before him visions which underlined the transitory nature of human life. The first vision was of Juana Andrea skating in the distance; and her shadow "that came from afar moved along the wall, and I felt it gliding over me like a breath, amorous but sad, because it came from another place and from other days." [15] With the arrival of this vaporous figure, he began then to see with the eyes of his heart. Still filled with jealousy, however, he sank into a second dream—a dream in which the world was diminutive, too small to contain both him and his rival. Still the hypocrite, in this dream he told Fulán that one of them must seek another world. They would toss a stone to see who must go. As the unsuspecting Fulán reached for the stone, Catito pushed his rival into the abyss. Catito now knew, however, that his action had been in vain, that he had added nothing to his happiness.

Casalduero, commenting on the adventure of the pigs in *El Quijote*, asserts that it is society which passes as a herd over the man who dreams of ideal life, that thus the naturalist or the positivist believes his vision of the world confirmed, but that it is the serenity of Don Quijote, insensitive to pain, that marks the difference between the baroque and

---

[14] *Ibid.*, 214.
[15] *Ibid.*, 230. This passage calls to mind the shadows in Plato's cave.

naturalism. The baroque ideal, he continues, is created in opposition to social and human reality. It does not hope to perfect or to eliminate reality; rather, to oppose it, to dominate it, and to make it submit.[16] Just as Don Quijote and Sancho have been defined as different rhythms, needing and opposing each other at the same time—the tense unity of two contradictory elements, "simulating that of the modern world" [17]—so it has proven to be with Fulán and Catito.

Too late, Catito realized that the shadowy presence of those we have betrayed lives on in our memory. Now "esta sombra ocupaba, entre nosotros, más espacio que antes aquel cuerpo." Now he understood that his ideal had gone beyond him and, with it, the peace he desired. For the first time thinking more of Fulán than of himself, he twisted and wove a rope of grasses as long as the depth of the abyss. To the rope he tied a little chair, from which floated a polka dot banner torn from the blouse of Juana Andrea. This chair he lowered into the depths of the void, hoping that Fulán would see and understand and would return from the abyss. "For now too late I had realized that all could have been remedied either by increasing the size of the world by means of magic or, by the same means, by proportionately reducing the size of our own bodies." Thus, Catito found his answer, if not peace. Casalduero might well have been writing of Fulán and Catito when he pointed out that, whereas Don Quijote's disillusionment was finally to be total, that of Sancho would be only partial. Just as Fulán received "una marca que se le estereotipó," so, too does Don Quijote represent the prototype of the ideal; and, therefore, both can find total disillusionment—total understanding. Both finally come to know that man must accept the reality of this world with all its goodness and all its imperfections, leaving for another,

---

16 Casalduero, 373.
17 Ángel Valbuena Prat, 79.

better world "las escencias puras." Sancho represents humanity, with its inherent weaknesses, and thus his disillusionment can be only partial. As Cervantes explained, "Since purely human affairs are not eternal, it is the essence of Sancho to approach the absolute as if it were the relative, the eternal as if it were the temporal."

Fulán, like Don Quijote, dies; and thus the two archetypes go beyond the confines of this world. But just as Sancho had become *quijotizado*, so has Catito gradually become *fulanado*. He gradually comes to understand the Erasmian idea that the temporal world should project the temporal beauty and love that can lead transcendently to the ideal.

With the sixth chapter, "Semifinal," the story comes to an end; but the novel itself was never finished. Perhaps this was only a literary artifice used by the author, who at one time had said that he intended to write a second part. Perhaps Hernández's adult life and death may be considered as the true ending. Certainly they would constitute a satisfactory one. Miguel de Unamuno wrote that he found in Sancho the earthly hope for humanity. May not the same be said of Catito? In reading the words which Unamuno addressed to Sancho and Don Quijote, one is struck by the figurative manner in which they may be applied, also, to Catito and Fulán. Indeed, the life of Hernández himself would appear to be the fulfillment of Unamuno's expressed hope. "Pobre Sancho," he wrote, "que te quedas sólo con tu fe, con la fe que te dió tu amo." Then he addressed himself to Don Quijote:

Sancho, que no ha muerto, es el heredero de tu espíritu, buen hidalgo, y esperemos tus fieles en que Sancho sienta un día que se le hincha de quijotismo el alma, que le florecen los viejos recuerdos de su vida escuderil, y vaya a tu casa y se revista de tus armaduras, ... y saque Rocinante ... y monte en él, y abrace tu lanza ... y ... salga al campo y vuelva a la vida de aventuras, convertido de escudero en caballero andante. Y entonces, don Quijote mío, entonces es cuando tu espíritu se asentará en la tierra. Es Sancho, es tu fiel Sancho, es Sancho el bueno, el que enloqueció cuando te curabas de tu locura en tu lecho de muerte, es Sancho el que ha de asentar para siempre el quijotismo sobre la tierra de los hombres. Cuando tu fiel Sancho, noble Caballero, monte en tu Rocinante, revestido de tus armas y abrazando tu lanza, entonces resucitarás en él y entonces se realizará tu ensueño. Dulcinea os cojerá a los dos, y estrechándoos con sus brazos contra su pecho, os hará uno solo.[18]

The Cervantine preoccupations are evident in the shorter prose works of Hernández, as well as in the major novel. The story within the story—*Abarca: Fragmento de novela*—was at first a part of *La paloma, el sótano y la torre*. In Hernández's *Obras* it is presented as a separate entity, following the novel. In spite of the realistic and, at times, naturalistic quality of the episode, this fragment, a presentation of an incident in the Mexican Revolution, is told in the manner and language characteristic of Hernández's prose. It is the story of a man who willingly sacrifices his life for a cause, the hopelessness of which does not for one moment deter him. The protagonist, Abarca, is, like Fulán and Don Quijote, the prototype of the ideal.

Addressing himself in the story to the spirit of man, Hernández wrote:

Y qué fuerzas sin ojos suelen ponerse en juego para encaminarte, que ni el ojo las ve ni el poseído por ellas las entiende. ¿De dónde nacen estas ideas absurdas que encajan al hombre por el camino recto, y lo hacen escoger las espinas mejor que el rodeo y la desviación? [19]

Hernández then emphasized the dedication of Abarca. "To the end, to solitude and even to death, he would transcend,

---

18 Unamuno, *Vida de don Quijote y Sancho, según Miguel de Cervantes Saavedra*, 251.
19 *Obras*, 250.

he would not be overcome. His course, his star, his compass, and his route lay straight ahead. Had anyone asked him why, he would not have known how to explain it." And just as with Abarca, he added, from time to time all men find themselves "in the midst of shadows and darkness." They, also, lack the words to explain the situation. "And so it is, however. Every man . . . finds at times that in his life there are no alternatives and that, of all the roads, his is the only one."

When Abarca had pushed himself to the limits of human endurance, he was finally forced to admit to himself, "I can do no more." These, of course, are the same words used by Don Quijote in the episode of the Enchanted Bark, when the knight errant finally felt himself utterly defeated in both the spiritual and the physical worlds. Abarca, like Quijote, well knew that there sometimes comes the moment when the die must be cast, when one must be true to one's self and to one's beliefs. When the final moment arrived, therefore, in which he was forced to choose between life and death, he struck the match without hesitation and held it to the dynamite fuse. Three days later, when the soldiers, his enemies, came to try again to capture him, they found that "the only path by which one could reach the mesa *or leave it* had been destroyed." Abarca had embraced his liberty. Having seen his power as a free moral agent and having accepted the glory and sorrow of that freedom, he chose to affirm his humanity with a destructive gesture of ultimate nobility.

More complicated is the short novel, *Cerrazón sobre Nicomaco: Ficción harto doliente*. It is the story of a man whose life from the beginning to the end is a failure because he never succeeds in synthesizing the dual planes of his nature. Nicomaco Estrellitas, the narrator and protagonist, lives very much in the politico-social world and is ostensibly dominated by reason. He is a man of some honor and a bureaucratic employee. Believing that his heart is overflowing with love for his wife and feeling that she is his whole world, he avoids close ties with anyone else. Indeed, he experiences a kind of love, but it is self-love; and this fact he never comes to realize. In the course of the story, Nicomaco, with all his complex psychological make-up—introspective, contemplative, intense—becomes for the reader a man of flesh and blood. The reader enters into his mind, his dreams, his fantasy, his philosophy, and his physical surroundings.

Nicomaco first reveals an overpowering conflict in his soul; then, in retrospect, he lives again the tragedy of his life. There are several fantastic and semi-fantastic episodes, as well as much social and political satire. The tragedy grows out of an unfounded jealousy he feels toward his wife. Finally, believing his doubts confirmed, his imagined rival takes the form of a kangaroo. The grotesque symbolism of the kangaroo underscores the absurd mania of Nicomaco. Because of her unselfish love for her husband and because of the suffering brought on by his overpowering dejection, his wife finally kills herself to prove his error to him. At the end of the novel, Nicomaco, convinced of his wife's innocence, yearns for death, knowing that this is the only avenue through which he can find peace.

To Nicomaco, water is the explicit correlative of intelligence, "humble, useful, precious, pure water," and he calls himself "the fool about water."

Soy el medio loco que nació para acabar de enloquecer al ver, oír, u oler el agua.

He aquí, soy el varón del agua; aquel cuyo destino si ya no es que haya comprendido mal a Dios, es llegar a ajustar en el dócil cristal cambiante de su versátil mano movediza, mi sortija.

Dentro del agua se halla todo el que no está en ella, como en la inteligencia. Como en la inteligencia, si se busca en el agua, se va encontrando más y más, indefinidamente.[20]

Thus within the water, as within the intelligence, the only thing one cannot see is the substance of the water itself, or of intelligence itself. The water calms him, but he does not know why. He cannot see the calming substance, that calming power which is within him, just as it is within the reflections in the water. "In spite of the black train formed by my great sins, within me there is something totally innocent that is not culpable." This "totally innocent something," however, he can never find. He has caught a glimpse of the ideal, of eternal mystery, in the water, just as he has glimpsed it in the eyes of his wife. In the water he can see only the reflection of his intelligence; in the eyes of his wife, only the type of love he has given her.

In his anxiety to understand, he sometimes feels that he catches a glimpse of truth:

... así como en la mente entra el dormir, a veces con ensueños, así, en el agua, entraba la tiniebla imaginando luces. Y sus luminiscencias se elevaban a tan imponderable contextura, que apenas creo temeridad pensar que más allá no debe ser sino el delgadísimo elemento de que está hecho el secreto impenetrable.

Oh, agua, que en tu simplicidad obtienes, para consuelo mío, tu transparencia. Pero ... ¿qué angel ha pasado? ¿Qué angel que no pasa y cómo, si no era como un río, ahora en un momento me ha dejado?[21]

He continues to feel that tenuous "innocent something" within himself; and in his anguish he turns to God. But his tragedy is that he has not "understood God"; he does not know the God of Love. Neither does he know of moral freedom. He chooses, rather, to believe that his individual responsibility lies in God's hands, and not in his own. Ad-

[20] *Ibid.*, 255. [21] *Ibid.*, 265.

dressing God, he announces, "It is certain that within me something has just broken; but it must be something of no importance. Had it been of any true worth, You above all would have understood it and would not have permitted its breaking." Finally, still unable to find a solution, this self-centered man concludes that he must be above normal men. "Now I only want to insist that, since I still have my sanity in spite of all the things that have happened to me, I must be immortal."

Now, even in the death which he visualizes and for which he yearns, he still plays the leading role. He sees himself draping the black material of mourning around the casket, arranging the funeral flowers, lighting the candles; and then:

... con polvorienta voluptuosidad, muy semejante a aquella con que levantamos hasta nuestros hombros las sábanas tibias, que nos aliviarán del afán constante del día, y de las impiedades de las impías noches de invierno, alzo y cierro la tapa.

Esta es ahora toda mi vida; y éste es ahora mi único sueño.[22]

This pitiful man, totally wrapped up in himself, is never to recognize the "quality of innocence" in his nature—the heart, the soul. He has refused to feel the pull, the affinity, between the two planes, with the consequence that he can never achieve humility, unselfish love, satisfaction, or peace. Casalduero's comment concerning the reign of Reason may also be applied to the life and death of Nicomaco: "It is the triumph of Don Diego de Miranda; it is the triumph of the limiting force"; because any genuine sentiment is absent, having been transformed "into philosophy and science." [23] Nicomaco is, in short, a point by point personification of the opposite of all that is noble in the character of Don Quijote.

How can the inspiration of the master Cervantes for Hernández best be summed up? Of direct allusion, there is little

---

[22] *Ibid.*, 274.   [23] Casalduero, 243.

to say. Hernández wrote no homages to Cervantes. Nor does he mount Fulán on a donkey, as an occasional modern Sancho appears. There are snatches of line, groups of words, that echo Cervantes. There are even identical phrases. Hernández's characters sometimes seem matched to Cervantes's eternal archetypes. And yet this comparison does not begin to describe the affinity between the two writers, for what Cervantes gave to Hernández (and to many other writers) is a way to think before the ostensible thinking begins. He contributed the terms and tools of Hernández's fiction, the presupposed values of his literary expression.

Chapter IV

THE POETRY:
ENTRE APAGADOS MUROS

ALTHOUGH HE BEGAN writing poetry before prose, Hernández's first collection of poems, *Hora de horas*, did not appear in print until 1935. In 1944 there appeared another volume, under the title, *Entre apagados muros*. This book included the poems of the first volume, many of them in a more polished version, plus several new ones. In his *Obras* there are seventeen poems under the division entitled "Entre apagados muros," and also seventeen under the division entitled "Otros poemas." Some of his poetry has never been published, and a few poems have appeared only in periodicals and newspapers. Two of the best known of the latter group are "El ángel del subsuelo" [1] and "Versos de una especie hoy no muy gustada." [2]

In an interview with María Luisa Mendoza, Hernández asserted that, although nobody knows exactly what poetry is, it is a necessity which sprouts from the very nature of man. He believed that the essence of poetry consists in the images which man projects of himself—images in which he expresses himself, recognizes himself, and finds peace. And he added that, just as if poetry were a mirror, its most pro-

[1] *Hoy*, July 15, 1939, 28.
[2] *América*, I, No. 50 (August, 1946), 45–46.

found imperative is that the image which it produces be the true reproduction of the object facing it.

In one definition he called poetry:

> ... una fuerza que se apodera del espíritu y lo convierte en instrumento de aprehensión y expresión de alguna realidad o sección de la realidad viva. Y a la autenticidad de esta realidad no admite otra comprobación que su capacidad de remover en cualquier tiempo a cualquier ser sensible, sin taras en su sensibilidad.[3]

And then he pointed out the close relationship between the one who writes poetry and the one who reads it. Striving for a more concise definition, he continued: "La poesía es el aliento que surge del silencio." [4]

In discussing the poets of Mexico, he stated that he believed José Gorostiza to be the best Mexican poet of the epoch. He called attention to an impressionist movement well underway, but not yet a truly great poetic movement, in his opinion. He expressed faith in the Mexican poets of his day and of the future, feeling that they would surpass those of the past. Among this latter group he believed that probably Sor Juana, el padre Pagaza, Gutiérrez Nájera, José Othón, Díaz Mirón, and López Velarde would be the ones whose work would endure. He refused to comment on Juan José Arreola and Octavio Paz, excusing himself by saying, "I do not want to hurt anyone." He named the German, Rilke, as the foreign poet whose work he preferred, and he named requiems as the type of music which held the greatest appeal for him.

Although Hernández's poetry is limited in quantity, critics are generally agreed that it is of very high quality. His poetic language is one of elegant simplicity, containing no folk elements; and his poetry—subjective, intimate, psycho-

[3] María Luisa Mendoza, 2, 4.
[4] *Ibid.*

logical—is usually pervaded by an atmosphere of solitude.

Among the poems in which he adhered to strict classical form are several sonnets and one *lira*—"Beatus ille." "Versos de una especie ..." is written in a free form of the *lira*, with lines of 11, 11, 11, 7, 7 syllables. Although he preferred lines of seven and eleven syllables, he also used lines varying in length from three to eighteen, with such disparity at times being found in the same poem. His stanzas vary in length from two lines to twenty, the length of each stanza being dependent upon, and limited by, the length of the one thought which it contains. He used both assonance and consonance in his more modern poetry.

Alfredo Cardona Peña writes that, although Hernández was not a classical poet in the true sense of the word—in the sense of strict meter and rhyme—his is "modern poetry, rich in classical ideas and emotions." [5] Octavio Novaro describes his poetry from the standpoint of meter and language as "tocado por la euritmia barroca de nuestros siglos de oro ... y para mi gusto moderno y para mi devoción verdadera a Efrén Hernández un poquitín trasnochada de siglos." [6] He hastens to add, however, that he is not so certain of the correctness of his judgments as was Hernández.

The title, "Entre apagados muros," is in itself intriguing. To explain the significance of the phrase ("between dim and dusty walls") is to describe the poetic content of the collection, analyzing in terms of the poetry the themes of dualism and mysticism, the motifs of hope and light, and the controlling idea of life. The way to an understanding of Hernández's poetry is neither short nor easy, for the good

[5] Cardona Peña, "Espejo de la voz: Efrén Hernández," *Novedades*, October 24, 1943, 2.

[6] Novaro, "Presencia de Efrén Hernández: Efrén Hernández o la inmodestia," *ibid.*, January 28, 1962, 3.

humor and popular irony of the prose is largely absent. Nonetheless, it is a fascinating journey and one that rewards the reader's patience and sympathy.

That dualism so characteristic of Hernández—the separation and harmony of the real and the ideal—is once again demonstrated in his poetry. In this dualism he gave evidence that he was in accord with the Gestalt approach to psychology, which holds that the corporeal and the psychic processes of living are interrelated and function together as a result of integrated units of stimuli. "What is intuition of whatever kind but the fruit of the harmonious and united operation of all our faculties?" [7]

As in his other works, so in his poetry, also, there is to be found the mystical influence—that mysticism which, according to Unamuno, succeeded in synthesizing the contradictions of the Spanish soul, that soul which "afirmaba ... dos mundos y vivía a la par en un realismo apegado a sus sentidos y en un idealismo ligado a sus conceptos. ..." [8]

In an article entitled "Algunos pensamientos que surgieron tratando de encontrar una definición de poesía," Hernández formulated some of his ideas concerning the unity and the mutability between these two planes. He believed that these two, the real and the psychic, alternately the *ser* and the *no ser*, between which man fluctuates, are the sources of the mystery of life. "Man is made up not only of his physical self with its intelligence; also within him is a mysterious subconscious world—essence—which determines him." [9] He defined intelligence as being to reality what the psychic is to infinity; memory, which is the remembering of

---

[7] Efrén Hernández, "Evocación de Horacio: Poema de Salomón de la Selva," 20.

[8] Miguel de Unamuno, *En torno al casticismo* (Madrid, 1895), 101.

[9] Efrén Hernández, "Algunos pensamientos que surgieron," 11, 16.

infinity, must then come through psychic knowledge. And thus he implied, although he did not state it, that the psychic is evidence of the soul.

He believed, in fact, that the soul is disturbed only by psychic objects, not by real objects. He believed, too, that the psychic, which functions in time but is freed from dimension and localization, thus possesses a certain quality of infinity. In his poetry, time and space are usually parallel to each other, but at times they merge into one. He pointed out that the psychic knows the present and, through memory, may dimly recall the past; and thus he could sense how one might imagine a type of existence defined in terms of existential philosophy—existence in which one must forge his own future. He believed that after the journey through this life, a journey filled with anxieties, yearnings, and hopes, man would pass to that other realm of eternal life with its harmonious silence, whose:

> ... especie no era sombra,
> ni su nombre era muerte,
> sino sonoridad ensimismada ... [10]

It was, characteristically, through both reason and sentiment that he achieved this feeling of hope.

"Tal vez no miro bien ..." invites the reader to accompany him along the path of Reason. In this poem he delivers a diatribe against Life, addressing it:

> Tal vez no miro bien, tal vez ha sido
> con yerba alguna amarga enhechizado
> mi seso, y lo he perdido;
> tal vez este vagar nunca entendido
> y divagar sin fin, me han atontado;
> tal vez tonto he nacido. ...
> . . . .

[10] *Obras*, 12.

pues yo no miro bien, pues yo he bebido,
pues me han con una yerba trastornado
los ejes del sentido,
o tú eres una pérfida ...

Si tuvieras de ser, lo que de bella,
si fueras algo más que no la pura
confluencia de la nada,
una pura ficción, una centella
volátil que no puede ser tocada,
ante el cielo entablara una querella
contra ti, en son de víctima engañada.

Oh, artera, oh, taimada,
¿qué es lo que pretendiste? ... [11]

He accuses Life of having brought man to an unknown
world and an unknown existence that man did not ask for;
of having united a delicate heart, a loving soul, and a dependent and trusting but limited intelligence with a mocking vision of beautiful things; and then of having put among
the splendors of the sensory world "this sensitive machine."
Finally feeling completely defrauded, he loses the mystical
illusion of faith. Now Life speaks with the voice of Reason
and explains how man has misunderstood, has lost the way.
She tells him to use all the "eyes" which she has given him:

Yo te di muchos ojos
—desde el topo hasta el ángel
te abrumé de evidencia—,
te di desde el opaco y ceguezuelo
lazarillo obscurísimo del tacto,
hasta la alada, fúlgida,
lustral y omnipresente inteligencia.

She accuses him of not having used his "eyes," of having
taken the echo for the noise, the sketch for the flower, the
shadow for the light.

[11] *Ibid.*, 35–36.

¿Conoces tú el conjuro
que sin la sombra la visión consiga,
la audición sin silencio,
el tacto sin el muro,
o de la inteligencia,
sin el nublado enigma, el fulgor puro?
. . . .
fallo en la sinrazón,
lo absurdo queda fuera
de mi jurisdicción.
. . . .
¿Y de este mirar tuerto
dirás, el imperfecto
e inconducente don, yo me lo he dado,
acaso me di yo mi inteligencia?
Yo, aquí, a la esperanza
que es condición perpetua
e inseparable cinto de tu esencia
te remito, ...

Life begs him not to be overcome by the things of this
world and then reveals her secret:

Por tanto, no te asombre ...
si en torno a ti, entre cactus
y lacertos y cruces, se va abriendo
boca de soledad, honda abertura
cada vez más desierta;
no es que de ti me aleje,
es que te abro la puerta. ...

Like the Renaissance Faust, Hernández yearned for more
light. In spite of his great reliance on reason for the answers to the unknown, he often showed his realization of
the weakness of the intellectual armor. In his desire to believe what reason would not let him believe, he poured out
his cry for faith in "Imagen de María":

Tus dulces ojos falsos,
fijos, brillantes, secos, de artificio
perfecto, necesarios

al hombre, que no saben
mirarse ni mirarnos
y parecen seguirme.
. . . .
Tu cuerpo que no añade peso al mundo.

Tú, la que eres casi, aunque no eres
otro que una forma
de grito, un hondo grito
de las entrañas huérfanas del hombre;
no pido que me mires
—ya sé que tú no miras—,
no pido que me oigas
—ya sé que tú no oyes—, enloquéceme,
hazme creer el encanto, solamente
hazme creer el encanto de que existes,
ciega mi entendimiento;
la luz, la necesito más
en el corazón.[12]

To his longer novel he gave the symbolic title which, along with the phrase, "Entre apagados muros," encompasses the meaning of all his poetic work, *el sótano* being symbolic of the sensory world—this "vil y baja tierra"—and *la torre* being symbolic of transcendental beauty, love, truth, while *la paloma* is the frail, imprisoned creature who must choose between the two. *Entre apagados muros,* the title of his volume of poems, is then simply a more poetic manner of expressing this same thought. The adjective *apagado* describes the condition caused by the dust—doubt or ignorance—which dims the light of hope, of faith. Whether this be dust from the sky or dust from the rooftops, it is still that "very subtle dust, which we call shadow. . . ."[13] At times it is man's reason which is caught between the *apagados* walls of his understanding; at times it is the soul caught between the *apagados* walls of man's sentiment. The author's struggle is to overcome this *apagada* condition lest:

[12] *Ibid.,* 15–17.   [13] *Ibid.,* 367.

> ... la esencia fija,
> ay, lo que cierto es, se oculta y huye;
> y el soplo encandesciente, el que a la corta,
> nimia forma de polvo, a la demente
> partícula apagada
> encendiera los ojos, ahora envuelto,
> cogido en vil corteza, entorpecido,
> en el mezquino seno
> de la viruta infiel, precisamente,
> que vino a iluminar, anda perdido.[14]

This, then, is the meaning of the title. Its significance illuminates, further, the major topics of Hernández's poetry: life, light, love, hope, and memory.

Life in this imperfect world was, to Hernández, a life of light and shadow, with the light, in Platonic fashion, representing the reflection of the eternal world and the shadow, the reflection of this world. Both his reason and his sentiment told him that here man is not abandoned; that he lives, rather, as a free moral agent between *apagados muros*; that it is he who causes the play between light and shadow. Often it is the sensory world which is the dimming medium; often it is man himself, as, with his back to the light, he contemplates his shadow. But still the light is there, the light from without, the light of ultimate truth, which comes to man through thought and reason. And the other light, the one from within, the light of the soul;

> Hondo, incomunicado,
> entre apagados muros,
> hay un recinto hermético, cerrado, fidelísimo,
> de libertad y paz,
> en realidad y luz, siempre encendido.[15]

This light must be felt instinctively, because:

> A esta región no aflige el movimiento;
> no la oye el oído, pues no vibra,

[14] *Ibid.*, 28.   [15] *Ibid.*, 31.

el tacto no la tienta, pues no oprime,
no la halla el pensamiento,
porque jamás se torna, ni las ondas
de la pasión la alcanzan, porque es simple,
inaccesible y pura.

De esta región no pueden
recibirse mensajes ...

It is to this search for light and hope that Hernández dedicated his poetic endeavors. He believed that, in this quest, man must be armed with resistance, patience, sincerity, and love; that man cannot know; but, in his desire for the light, he is capable of elevating the institution of hope to a level that is both inspiring and intellectually respectable. Light and hope become fused in the poetry, with the result that light itself is addressed in a novel way:

Para tu luz, mi cuerpo
se abrió como el cristal, ...

Todo es tuya la estancia de mi cuerpo; ...
todos los corredores,
todas las galerías,
todas las escaleras y caminos
de mi cuerpo se llaman casa tuya.

. . . .
Mi casa, cual sin puertas,
mi cuerpo cual sin alma,
mi alma, cual sin Dios,
así te han aceptado, ...

. . . .
... mi cuerpo entra al rezumante
y cristalino mundo del rocío,
que alcanzó las montañas, que las dejó,
que atrás queda la cárcel,
entre caídas cosas
de peso y pesadumbre,
para siempre caída y olvidada.[16]

[16] *Ibid.*, 42–43.

Such lines indicate that Hernández has accepted at least
the terminology of a transcendental, perfect world. Attain-
ing that realm involves all the traditional problems associ-
ated with philosophical dualism. It is hardly surprising that
the way to that realm should be expressed through the vocabulary of Plato, Sartre, and Carlyle. Nor is it extraordi-
nary that light should become both the goal and the way, or
that an emphasis on love should inform the whole scheme, so
that hope, light, and love should be poetically mingled. He
supposed that light must lead the way to love; that the human soul, without light, is in absolute disarray, like

> ... el pez etincelante
> que en limo hondo y vago, abajo hundido,
> como una luz ya quieta se ha parado; ...

Only very infrequently does a little light, a little understanding, come to this soul in disarray: "Sólo de tiempo en
tiempo, ... / suelen abrirse un poco mis nublados." But however difficult this type of love may be for the human soul,
it is the type toward which the soul has a natural affinity:

> ... el alma entera es suelta, leve y blanda,
> amor, pero te quiso,
> pero te quiso, amor, y aunque hoy te quiera
> débil y pobremente,
> te quiere según puede y según puede
> quisiera retenerte. ... [17]

Along the road to love, selfishness is not allowed to pass;
thus man must forget himself:

> Lo mismo que la gota
> bajo la abnegación, así la pena
> suya es barrida y rota
> de pronto, y ya no llena
> su ser sino el combate de la ajena.
>
> . . . .

[17] *Ibid.*, 33.

Y ahí el número empieza,
que ignora una unidad, que ni termina,
ni sabe la tristeza
que al hombre contamina,
desde que en sí, fundado, se imagina.

This love he describes as a broken smile upon the lips or
as tears glistening in the eyes:

... porque al que siente amor,
porque al que siente
de inundación de amor ...

.   .   .   .

en turbación se ahoga
y en ahogo náufraga y enmudece,
o no es amor de amores,
el amor del mar de amor —mar de los mares—
ni amor de mis amores el que siente.

Oh urgente y muda voz,
oh muda voz de amor, incontenible
y fracasada siempre.

Oh inmensa voz de amor, voz invencible
y derrotada siempre[18]

In "A Beatriz," a poem dedicated to his wife, the transcendental quality of romantic love is underscored.

Oh, devoción recíproca,
función ultraterrena que sublima
los jugos de la carne y torna templo
de comunión, la médula profunda.[19]

In the woman he loves, man senses the ideal for which he
yearns.

Mi vida mira a ti, como una torre
con la ventana tensa, y en su obscuro
antro de soledades en silencio
pasa, como fantasmas, en angélico
proceso, el pormenor de tus acciones.[20]

[18] *Ibid.*, 50.   [19] *Ibid.*, 13–14.   [20] *Ibid.*, 13.

All these thoughts close in upon him at night when she is sleeping, and:

> Ésta es la hora amante y amarguísima,
> en que mi vida se alza entre la noche
> y vaga en una torre imaginaria.

And in answer to his intuitive yearning, out of his love for Beatriz comes hope.

If the reader allows himself to be carried by Hernández's account of man's tortuous journey through this world—this journey between "apagados muros"—he can follow step by step the poet's manner of resolving the polarity, the duality, of which man is the victim.

Hernández describes the frail creature, man, as a bubble: "... la inmensamente frágil / monada y nihilidad de una burbuja. ..."[21] Armed with reason, this bubble lives and floats upon the "invincible, laborious, patient hammerings of the blood," which it must fear, since the marking of the passage of time is also a repeated message telling the limits of reason. If man had total understanding, he would require no temporal dimension to achieve infinitude. If he had unlimited time, his reason would attain infinite understanding. Time is, then, simultaneously the glorious medium in which reason operates and also the unwanted check on reason.

> Pero la sangre, en sujeción a ocultas
> servidumbres selladas,
> y, en secreto, operario
> agente de escondidos
> y nunca pronunciados pensamientos,
> conmovedoramente
> y por entero dada
> y consagrada a su trabajo, quiere
> que la burbuja oiga,
> que el punto se enderece,
> que el cascarón soporte,

[21] *Ibid.*, 68.

> que se establezca el átomo
> en permanencia, y oiga. Y la burbuja
> se mueve a obedecer; pero no acierta
> a oír, no acierta a oír ...
> Que ella más quisiera
> romperse ya,
> romperse. ... Que eso es
> lo que ella sabe:
> romperse. ... [22]

In the poem, "Soneto en que se previene al alma los peligros de asomarse al jardín de la belleza," Hernández warns man against the temptations of this world: In a moral and esthetic Eden, man must exercise restraint. The poem warns against the temptation of the temporal, sensory world and affirms that man must rely on the human equivalent of infinite understanding in order to achieve truth. The equivalent is faith.

> Pues en verdad venimos
> de lejos
> y en verdad vamos lejos.
> Tan lejos, que no puede
> llegar el pensamiento
> tan lejos. Y tampoco
> nuestras más negras lágrimas, y
> antiguas, e infinitas,
> y enormes, que nosotros.
>
> Más lejos, aún más lejos que aquel monte,
> casi fuera del mundo,
> que ya se mira azul, está la luna;
> más que la luna, el sol, y más lejano
> que la más tenue estrella, está el instante
> cuyos talones pisan
> este nuevo que ahora
> en solo imagen señalar intento
> y, a su vez, huye ya.[23]

[22] *Ibid.*   [23] *Ibid.*, 53–54.

And man must remember that, in reality, time and distance are dimensions of his reason, dimensions which are ultimately unimportant.

In connecting the temporal and transcendental realms, Hernández has resorted to the phenomenon which fascinated Wordsworth, Proust, and Rilke—that human capacity called memory. Through it, man may perhaps come to know eternity, which Hernández describes poetically as "the abyss . . . the open mouth of silence. . . ."[24] Because memory is a part of eternity;

> Tu parte fue la noche,
> tu origen las orillas,
> tu antecedente, tú, lejos de ti
> —yo aún sin esperanza, lejos, lejos—
> y tu nido el abismo.[25]

Then memory comes to man:

> Y al encantado golpe,
> preciso, que sentí, bajé hasta el fondo;
> mas ya caí, no huyendo,
> no, sino encontrándome.
>
> Y no fui como el ciego a quien un día
> sonríe el dón de la luz;
> mas, como una memoria
> perdida, que retorna.[26]

And thus memory becomes the connecting thread which links this world with eternity. It becomes the light that illumines man's soul so that man must suffer no longer "la más llorosa de todas mis heridas, ... que es la que está más lejos de la luz. ..."[27] And memory, having brought man light, now also introduces hope into his soul:

> Entero te me di, y vi en tus ojos
> de pronto a mis espaldas disolverse

24 *Ibid.*, 67.
25 *Ibid.*, 47.

26 *Ibid.*, 48.
27 *Ibid.*, 66.

el peso de mi cruz, mi carga oscura
y mi aflicción cesar y desatarse,
tornarse a un blando influjo en suave ensueño
y convertirse en ala.[28]

Finally hope has given wings to the soul; and the heart and the soul of man can coexist:

Y ya en presencia puesto,
sin peso el corazón, sin intermedio,
cabe tus pies graciosos,
a tu figura intacta, a tu hermosura,
el ansia ya sin vuelo,
colmado el anhelar
y la ambición vencida,
ya cosa a que aspirar no concibiendo,
ninguna demandaron, entendieron
que todo era ya suyo, que en ti estaban
la propia inmensidad, la luz, el aire,
los permanentes ramos que las rosas
efímeras envían, vagarosas,
de los cambiantes sueños; del abismo
el fondo y la cubierta, las rondanas
del tiempo, la delgada
vereda por do huyen, la cabaña
perdida en donde paran
y, al borde de su río, al fin descansan.[29]

Thus does Hernández poetically resolve the duality and point the way to success in man's quest for the ideal.

To understand the poetic solutions to the problems posed by philosophical dualism, Hernández can be advantageously compared to a number of other poets. Such comparison is helpful in determining the place of Hernández in the history of literature. Perhaps the most striking similarities of poetic expression are to be observed in the respective works of Hernández and Antonio Machado. This comparison seems natural, considering the similarities between the poetic and

[28] *Ibid.*, 48.   [29] *Ibid.*, 48–49.

the philosophical natures of the two writers. Each dedicated himself to the search for the quintessence of the Spanish spirit. Like Hernández, Machado had belonged to no literary movement, in spite of the profound influences on him of modernism and the Generation of 98. Beneath the surface of the poems of Machado—also a writer of classical bent, deeply influenced by Horace and Fray Luis—there also surge turbulent waters. The literary production of both holds appeal for the educated reader. In spite, however, of the quality of the popular in his prose writings, Hernández cannot be classified as a *populista* or *folklorista*, as is Machado. The two were in accord that man, in his seeking for a more perfect life, cannot create a world apart but, rather, must stay on the side of other men and fight for the better life. Machado, like Hernández, felt abiding love for his fellows—individual men—and to each of them the idea of the masses degraded the throngs of men. Both had their alter egos, through whom they expressed their philosophical attitudes; and such qualities as determination, religious inquietudes, and humility were common to both. Federico de Onís, in his introduction to a work on Machado by Gabriel Pradal-Rodríguez, might well have been writing of Hernández when he described Machado as "one who within his solitude, in memory, and in the galleries of his soul searches for the mystery of the eternal. . . ." [30]

The themes of memory, the dream, the unknown, the *ignorabimus*, the meaning of time—all these and more are common to the works of both. Machado, in whose poetry time is the essential theme, was greatly influenced by Berg-

[30] Gabriel Pradal-Rodríguez, *Antonio Machado (1875–1939): Obra y vida—Bibliografía—Antología—Obra inédita*, with an intro. by Federico de Onís, Hispanic Institute in the United States (New York: Casa Hispánica of Columbia University, 1951), 10.

son's ideas on the subject. According to Bergson, the man of intuition is, indeed must be, a creature of time, but not of time which the watch records or which the intellect divides into seconds, minutes, or hours. Rather, this man is a creature of what Bergson called *la durée*, a process carried on by memory. Thus intuition and memory grasp the basic nature of the flow of time, the flow of consciousness. Hernández's poetry is filled with this same idea—this sense of the past in the present which is becoming the future. Hernández and Machado both believed that poetry must be on the plane of psychic *temporalidad* and that the language must be chosen not only for its literal meaning but also for its symbolic interpretation. The danger of illusions was in the thoughts of both: in the work of Machado, eyes are the prominent symbol for the double image; in that of Hernández, water.

Symbology raises the problem of style, a topic worthy of separate consideration. Before turning to an analysis of style, however, the reader would do well to observe in Hernández's poetry a peculiar quality that is uniquely his and that is difficult to describe. The quality is quiet heroicism, wise and restrained optimism. It can be seen in his last poem, published after his death and entitled "De una vez despidámonos." In this beautiful sonnet, classical in form, the poet, hoping to find that better life, bids goodbye to this one:

> De una vez despidámonos, no fuera
> a acontecer después, que como vino,
> sin saludar, marchárase el destino,
> cuando mi adiós decir ya se pudiera.
>
> Ya el sol para caer bien poco espera.
> Ya a su fulgor contemplo, mortecino,
> descalza, sin su carro y ya en camino,
> de espaldas hacia mí la primavera.

Ya este existir no tiene, simplemente,
mayor cosa que ver con estas cosas.
Todo ha de ir trocándose en ruinas.

¿En dónde está el jardín del cual se cuente:
Aquí de noche y en invierno hay rosas,
nunca se van de aquí las golondrinas? [31]

---

[31] *Obras,* 83–84.

Chapter V

THE STYLE

FOR A MAN OF the twentieth century bent on dealing simultaneously with rationality and imagination, the simple act of expression can loom as an incredible obstacle. T. S. Eliot saw the problem of literary expression in an age of scepticism when he wrote:

> Words move, music moves
> Only in time; but that which is only living
> Can only die, Words, after speech, reach
> Into the silence. Only by the form, the pattern,
> Can words or music reach
> The stillness, as a Chinese jar still
> Moves perpetually in its stillness.
> Not the stillness of the violin, while the note lasts,
> Not that only, but the co-existence,
> Or say that the end precedes the beginning,
> And the end and the beginning were always there
> Before the beginning and after the end.[1]

Here, the dilemma becomes the topic of poetry, but the topic is, after all, limited; and were the dilemma the sole topic, then poetry would have arrived at a sorry state.

Writers who purport to deal with the truth, as Hernández did, must cultivate a complex of key devices—motifs,

[1] *The Complete Poems and Plays, 1900–1950* (New York: Harcourt, Brace, and World, 1962), 121.

symbols, figures, and referents—which carry a meaning that is more significant than quotidian reality. To observe Hernández's cultivation of his special poetic garden tells much about the man and, of course, describes much about his artistic tools.

With Hernández, prose and poetry are but two manifestations of the same deep yearnings and anxieties, and certain stylistic characteristics are to be found in both his prose and his poetry. With the exception of the first poem in *Entre apagados muros*, the whole of his artistic work is directed "to the lover who has fallen upon misfortune," to the "exiled one," who has lost his firm and easy faith:

> ... y ahora suelto,
> vacante, a la deriva,
> viudo, vienes hablando, dando cuenta,
> monologando siempre, y no descansas
> tu soliloquio urdiendo.
> He aquí, yo sé quién eres,
> mejor que a mis tristezas te conozco;
> tu eres igual a mí, ven, hablaremos.[2]

Here he also gives the clue to his manner of expression in both his prose and his poetry—his thoughts pour forth in agonizing soliloquies and monologues.

In unedited notes he wrote concerning language:

Decir que el lenguaje es un medio de expresión equivale a decir que el hablar es un medio de hablar. El lenguaje es un medio de conocimiento ... el vehículo que hace posible el pensar y hace posible el primer pensamiento de donde se va entrando después a otros pensamientos. ... Por lo tanto si el arte es "la expresión del universo a través del hombre," el lenguaje como arte debe determinar al hombre, y el hombre está constituído no solamente por lo físico y razonable, en su vida se encierra un mundo misterioso, subconciente que lo determina.[3]

[2] *Obras*, 9–10.
[3] Cited by Bosque Lastra, 27.

All his thoughts seemed to lead him to this mysterious world, this world beyond reason; and the words with which he chose to picture this world have been described as *añejas*, like old and precious wine.[4] Villaurrutia explains that his love for the classical works of the Siglo de Oro led him to a language somewhat archaic and so unused that to the modern reader it seems almost as if it were new.[5] To some extent his use of such language may also be related to the fact that, even until today in his native state of Guanajuato, many archaic words and expressions still survive and are to be found in the familiar speech.[6]

Just as in his life and in the philosophical content of his work, so, too, in his style he wanted to maintain the balance between the ideal and the real; he searched for the stylistic position where "from below rose the noise of the city; from above fell the silence of the universe." [7] In his manner of writing he often makes time and eternity merge, just as, in strolling through the Zócalo one night, his mind confuses the yellow moon with the lighted face of the town clock.[8]

To choice of words, Hernández gave great care and thought. Mallén writes that he cultivated them so delicately it seemed as though he were afraid that he was going to harm them.[9] One critic, in referring to the tender bitterness which pervades his short stories, says that it emanates not from the words themselves but from, ". . . the very vitals of each of the letters in the words." [10] Hernández called the

---

[4] Manuel Lerín, "Literatura en Efrén Hernández," *América*, I, No. 32 (December, 1944), 24.

[5] Xavier Villaurrutia, "El señor de palo," 14–15.

[6] See Bosque Lastra, 53.

[7] *Obras*, 279.

[8] *Ibid.*, 295.

[9] Rubén Salazar Mallén, "La muerte de Efrén Hernández," *El Universal*, February 4, 1958, 3.

[10] Clemente López Trujillo, "Efrén Hernández, cuentista," *El Nacional*, October 18, 1941, 3.

word the bread of the thought. "It nourishes the whole thought by entering into its blood stream and pervading it throughout." [11] For Hernández words led the way to the expression of the mind and of the soul. He knew, however, the difficulty of finding with words the pathways into the realm of the soul:

> Mal con palabras puedes
> —piezas de agitación—,
> ni con móvil guía de inconstantes
> y locos pensamientos, conducirte
> al frágil, fino alcázar
> que edificar no saben sino sólo
> las laboriosas manos de silencio.[12]

In phrases reminiscent of both T. S. Eliot and Rilke, the reader comes to know his poetic idea of eternity: the realm of silence and stillness, the nothingness or transparency of clear water. He felt that in the world of memory there must have been words of a sort different from that of normal discourse.

> Antes de hoy, es cierto,
> palabras que no son a semejanza
> de la arrojada piedra, se dijeron,
> que sin turbar ni el filo
> de una tela de araña, se allegaron
> sumáronse a la gracia, se empaparon
> en el divino espejo;
> pero eran de otra suerte,
> surcaron otros aires,
> cayeron de otro mundo.

From the Bible he quotes: "De lo que el corazón abunda, habla la boca ... ," then asks:

> ... de lo que le falta,
> eso de que carece,

---

[11] Efrén Hernández, "Algunos pensamientos que surgieron," 11.
[12] *Obras*, 19.

de lo que está vacío y tiene hambre
¿no es también, por ventura,
de donde toman vena y se abastecen
su canto y su clamor? [13]

He came to believe that, of all the kinds of words, it is not those spoken by reason or by the empty heart, but those spoken by the heart filled with love, beauty, and faith, that can lead one to the "princely dwelling" which only the "hands of silence" know how to build.

Hernández seems to have agreed with Heraclitus that everything begins with water. His whole literary output abounds with the meanings of its various qualities and states. Just as man represents the blending of the real and the ideal; just as his work is the blending of "myth and history," of ideal perfection and reality—antithetical poles, according to the neo-Aristotelian *Poética*—so, too, does water represent these same oppositions. Its simplicity, he feels, lies in its transparency; but this transparency is present only in calm, clear water on which light falls. And it is only occasionally that water is found in this completely peaceful state. Therefore, water is, in general, complex, not simple, just as Hernández's symbolism concerning water is usually very complex.

With him the properties of water acquire transcendental qualities. He compares lights in dark water with dreams in the sleeping mind; and in both, he believes, is the "very delicate element of which the impenetrable secret is made." [14] At times he sees water as the link between man and eternity: "They say that in Paradise below there was much water. . . . And God himself found infinite peace there. . . ." [15] On other occasions he draws the comparison between water and the soul, as when he asserts that the self-reliant soul, like water, seeks its own level, thus achieving "freedom to flow,

[13] *Ibid.*, 20.   [14] *Ibid.*, 265.   [15] *Ibid.*, 256.

to follow its natural course, to tend toward what it is." [16] At other times water is like truth—"strong, terrible, powerful, invincible." [17] Like truth, it overcomes all obstacles; and to prevail against it is as impossible as for an ant to move a mountain or for a person to outdistance his shadow or to raise himself from the ground by an upward tug on his hair.

He can equate water with life. It is the lack of water which causes the dryness of the desert, thirst in the body, and sin in the soul. Its presence brings greenness and purity. Hernández claims that for him it has a calming effect, while at the same time it revitalizes him. He sways with the motion of this life-giving liquid and seems to find his destiny in "the gentle, changing mirror of its constantly moving hand . . ." [18] It is only when the darkness is so deep that man's shadow abandons him and man is left in the state of mortal shock and agony that the life-giving properties of water are lost. In such a state the water turns to blood, "my soul saw itself bathed completely in blood . . . ," [19] and death is the only consolation.

The real qualities of water—its ability to sustain and to overcome, to build and to destroy—are symbolically presented in a fairly straightforward manner. But even on the real plane, Hernández presents the antithetical poles which water represents. Not only does it mirror true reflections; it also produces *espejismos*, or false images. On its surface there may be smoothness and peace, light, life, serenity, and depth. But underneath, where the eye—impeded by false reflections—cannot see, snakes, worms, and frogs hide, and the earth is decayed.

Throughout his work the reflection of eternity is often symbolized by a mirror, a glass, a pool, backed with quicksilver and alive with pure light. When dust—the things of

[16] *Ibid.*, 187.
[17] *Ibid.*, 149.
[18] *Ibid.*, 255.
[19] *Ibid.*, 267.

this world—strikes this mirrored surface, the quality of its reflection is upset and distorted; and man "can see himself only in still water." [20] But most often it is the fountain which represents the reflection of eternity, the eternity of memory, by which man in this world may have an intuitive idea of the future world; it represents the mirror, or calm water, in which man may catch a glimpse of himself and of ultimate truth.

> ... pero el pasado es fuente y, aun ausente,
> su palpitada esencia me conmueve,
> me turba como un germen, como un rastro,
> como una cruel raíz retrocedida
> que no llegó a soñar su sueño inmenso;
> y nos la dió a nosotros.[21]

This fountain is "happy, silent and remote beneath a mirror in the midst of solitude"; and the mirror of the fountain represents the conscience that gradually becomes still and finally sees itself clearly. In this fountain are the "eternal two faces."

... Sino que en la fuente hay dos espejos, éste de afuera en donde se copia el cielo, y el interno en que se dureciendo, nos permitiese cobijarla con un párpado de azogue, espejo en que si la fuente tuviese el ojo de la mente, se miraría a sí misma y a sí mismo desde abajo, espejo de la sabiduría, de la conciencia de la autociencia.[22]

The *cuenca* is not only the socket of the eye. In the work of Hernández it is also the valley of eternity glimpsed by the eyes of the soul; and in these eyes tears are "the poorest dew to which a soul in its extremes of dryness can aspire." [23]

If water is perhaps the most complex and pervasive of his poetic referents, the word *tren* is perhaps the most confus-

---

[20] Efrén Hernández, "Sobre lo humano en la poesía," *América*, I, No. 21 (October, 1943), 32.
[21] *Obras*, 13.   [22] *Ibid.*, 393.   [23] *Ibid.*, 12.

ing. By *tren* he designates two processes: the train of life
and time, and the train of man's yearning, desires, and anxieties. Always the hyperconscious user of words, he explains:

> Hay un choque ... entre estos dos trenes dialécticos que van en
> encontradas direcciones. ... La llamita del tiempo va corriendo;
> va corriendo sobre el hilo de la mecha hacia la bomba ... .
> En todo buen concierto, en todo buen discurso, en toda buena
> máquina todos los movimientos deben ser caminantes en un solo
> sentido, y todas las tendencias, entenderse bien, e ir, como de la
> mano, hacia una sola meta. ...[24]

Hernández's answer to the danger of the collision of these
two trains is, not unexpectedly, love, for only love can en-
dow everything with perfect beauty and unify all things,
so that "todo cuanto existe y el cielo, son lo mismo." [25]

Occasionally, within a story or poem, Hernández paints
a word picture in vivid colors:

> ¡Ay negra, negra suerte! Qué esquiliano espectáculo reco-
> gieron mis ojos; tal como si el campeón de los aparadoristas los
> hubiera dispuesto así quedaron. Hubierais visto el pliego guinda,
> desplegado, aletear airoso sobre un macizo de amapolas amari-
> llas; el medio litro de lámina cromada, con su asa naranja, de pie
> sobre el único remiendo negro de un pavimento de mosaicos
> marfilinos, y en medio de los tres dobledecímetros en posición
> de flechas encargadas de encaminar los ojos hacia él, y una mano
> a mano de guantes escarlata, con violetas, brillando como brasas
> sobre las que soplara un fuelle, encima de, precisamente, el cés-
> ped más tupido y verde que se podía encontrar en cien metros a
> la redonda. ...[26]

José Rojas Garcidueñas describes this as a "delicate paint-
ing," which, because of its plastic elements, suggests somewhat the work of Dali, although the colors here are more
vivid. He feels, also, that it is reminiscent of the work of
Juan Miró.[27]

---

[24] *Ibid.*, 253.   [25] *Ibid.*, 377.   [26] *Ibid.*, 259–60.
[27] J. R. Garcidueñas, "Notas sobre tres novelas mexicanas," *Anales del
Instituto de Investigaciones estéticas*, XVI (1943), 12.

In Gracián's *El Criticón*, as Andrenio is led through the world by Critilo, he travels through the "four seasons" of life: (1) springtime, or childhood; (2) the flower-filled summer, or youth; (3) the season of mature fruits, autumn, or that of the mature years; and (4) that season of coldness and sadness, winter, or old age. In "El señor de palo," Hernández presents in colors the same four stages in the life of Domingo, the protagonist:

Pasó primero por la rosada infancia, pasó, en seguida, por la roja juventud, y por la madurez morada, a la que siguió su anochecer; quedando al fin de las cuentas, aclarado que lo que pareció un teñir, fue en realidad un desteñir, y la apariencia de un vivir, un ir muriendo.[28]

Whether the chromatic element be indistinct or vivid, there is frequently a poetic blending of colors, unless it is pure white which pervades the landscape. This pure white represents the perfect harmony of color, of eternal hope, and seems to correspond to clear water.

> Ella no es nada verde,
> no es verdad que sea verde.
> Ni siquiera sus ropas
> son del color que sólo
> después del que reserva
> el cielo para sí, aman los ojos.
>
> El más puro entre todos,
> el blanco ... [29]

Throughout his work, Hernández resorts to chiaroscuro when he writes of color, just as he does when dealing with psychological concerns. More than one critic has called Hernández's prose works poetic epigrams. In his prose there is at times the same succinctness of sentence structure to be found in the epigrammatic prose of Gracián. Very frequently, however, the wandering, monologic manner of

[28] *Obras*, 340. [29] *Ibid.*, 80.

Hernández's prose does away with concision of thought, just as the deceptively clear sentences of Gracián are often obscure in meaning. Bustamente recalls that, in a conversation with his friend, Hernández had once expressed the fear that the worth of his literary work had been weakened by this "ingenua elegancia de su estilo que le es ineludible" [30] and by the fact that his irony had not been sufficiently bitter.

The customary manner of his narration may be described by one short sentence in "Tachas": "Yo hablaba como si estuviera solo, monologando." [31] From time to time, however, he deviates from the monologue, or soliloquy, and speaks directly to the reader, addressing him as *lector, tú,* or *usted*; occasionally he speaks to *vosotros* or to *ustedes*. And sometimes, he explains, "usted, para mí, no significaba nadie ... absolutamente nadie. Era el personaje imaginario, con quien yo platico cuando estoy a solas."

While in his poetry Hernández maintains esthetic distance, in his prose he greatly reduces the distance. At times the reader almost feels that he himself becomes a part of the story:

> ¿Se ha fijado usted, lector, en que cuando se encuentra en una postura perfectamente cómoda, si algo viene a distraerle y usted se mueve, cuando intenta volver a acomodarse se encuentra con que ya no es posible por nada del mundo? [32]

Occasionally he breaks the thread of his story to tell a joke or to add some other light and humorous touch, such as the following passage: "En este momento me parece a mí ser pertinente tender un entreacto para dar lugar al reposo necesario ... ." [33] In truth, the tense situation to which he refers has been serious only for the protagonist; the reader, on the other hand, has been amused, both by the situation and by the manner of its presentation.

[30] O. Bustamente, "A la carta: Homenaje a Tachas," 6.
[31] *Obras*, 280. [32] *Ibid.*, 294. [33] *Ibid.*, 297.

The *humorismo* in Hernández's work is at times sharp, like that of Gracián; more often, however, it is of a kindlier and more gentle type. This style does not conceal from the reader that Hernández is dealing with serious things. It is only an artifice, in which the obvious theme, which seems innocuous and of little depth, is less perturbing than the true theme, which may be perceived unfolding beneath the surface of the story.[34]

In the short story, "Santa Teresa," an unimportant little mouse appears and disappears, tries to nibble at a shoestring and then, playing dead, leads the mind of the protagonist to the "raposita mortecina de la fábula del conde Lucanor":

"Si pasara un home, e dijera que los pelos de la frente del ratón es bueno poner los en la frente de los niños para que no los aojen, él permanecería quieto como la raposita. Pero pues no pasa ningún home; ningún home dice nada, ningún home saca tijeras para cortar los pelos de la frente del ratón.

"Un refrán indica: cree el león que todos son de su condición. En este refrán, león no quiere decir únicamente león, sino Pedro, Juan o Francisco. Por eso, al ratoncito se la prende en la imaginación una malicia, y descubre que yo también me estoy haciendo el muerto."[35]

This in turn leads his mind to the fable of the country mouse and the city mouse, and social satire grows out of the consideration. He now projects himself into the mind of the mouse. Since to men all mice look alike, so to mice, he reasons, all humans must look alike. Santa Teresa, who in the form of a picture is hanging on the wall, has never been a threat to the mouse; therefore, this other human is probably another Santa Teresa and should pose no threat to him, either. And the little mouse, at whom he has kicked once, approaches again without fear.

[34] See the comments of Alberto Bonifaz Nuño, "El cuentista Efrén Hernández," *Novedades*, March 23, 1952, 3.

[35] *Obras*, 286–87.

In Hernández's prose, plot is unimportant, at times almost totally lacking. A master of the miniature, he seems to be in his natural element when he writes of unimportant things, "otorgándoles la paradójica transcendencia de que en la vida hay sólo una cosa importante: la cosa que no tiene importancia." [36] In his desire for detail, for the miniature, for "lack of transcendence," Hernández put into his work nothing of exaggerated emotion, little of the heroic, nothing starkly tragic, no blaring noises or gross violence, and few animated posturings or gestures. He strove, rather, for simplicity, and his work at times almost seems to have been written in a minor key.

Dialogue and movement are almost absent. The narrator characterizes himself as a wanderer who travels, in monologues, the highways and the byways of his soul, at times touching the main road, more often detouring in various directions. There seems to be no deliberate purpose, no planned technique. It is frequently difficult to find the elements which relate to the central theme. All the wanderings, however, finally reunite.

This method is well illustrated when Hernández, through the protagonist in "El señor de palo," represents man, the paralytic, traveling on the train of life, "el tren de por los siglos de los siglos;" "y si el sujeto de la acción del verbo ir en tren, es soñador, no podrán contarse los castillos en el aire que fabrica, ni los primores con que los adorna." [37] As Domingo, the protagonist, he explains his narrative technique:

Eleazar Noriega me dijo, precisamente hace unos días, lo que ahora creo adivinar en el pensamiento del lector. Tú, me dijo, disertas con muy buena ilación, pero de repente sales con grandísimas distancias y lo dejas a uno hecho un tarugo.

Creo que Noriega no deja de tener razón, pero sólo dentro de

[36] José Luis Martínez, "Efrén Hernández," *Novedades*, July 8, 1962, 3.
[37] *Obras*, 315.

él; dentro de mí, yo también tengo razón. Dentro de mí, el pensamiento obedece a una estricta concatenación, nada más que a veces es extraordinariamente rápido y las palabras que lo vierten no alcanzan a seguirlo y sólo expresan los nudos más salientes.[38]

His thoughts move with ease from the shortness of life to the length of the bedroom: "Life is too short and the room is too long . . . ,"[39] and from the window to the cloud. His mind travels, also, from the distractions of life to the absolute world beyond.

Such narrative meandering is not an unconscious trait. Hernández recognized within himself an element of the picaresque, a clinging to the simple flow of events in time. He developed the trait and used it for purposes of humor, but he also exploited the picaresque toward more serious ends. In the novel, *La paloma, el sótano y la torre*, the protagonist, looking back to his childhood wrote: "Me conocía harto pícaro y harto mosca muerta y mátalas callando ... , y precisamente en estas malas propiedades basaba mi satisfacción, y en estas dotes, en rigor negativas, ponía toda mi complacencia."[40] Hernández seems to have recognized his own childhood in that of the protagonist; but as the poet grew older and as there developed more harmony between his head and his heart, this wandering quality began to change, to become less negative, to verge more toward mere mischievousness and, curiously enough, stoicism. However, in 1937, in a letter to a friend, Hernández still demonstrated a preoccupation concerning this perversity: "Me estorba mi malicia, me hace pensar burlas, que son fruto de torear, del evadir, de no poder compenetrarse y comprender."[41] This attribute, a product of his intellect, his reason, gradually came to be held in check by the innate kindness which pro-

---

[38] *Ibid.*, 326.　　　[39] *Ibid.*, 282.　　　[40] *Ibid.*, 91.
[41] Efrén Hernández, "Carta a Alfredo Maillefert," *Letras de México*, November 15, 1937, 3.

ceeded from his heart; and critics are agreed that Hernández succeeded in converting an essentially negative quality into a positive one that enabled him to find the way to make fun even of his own thought. Out of such interplay emerged the quality of *humorismo*, that mixture of wit and irony, of sadness and joy, which stands out as one of the most distinctive characteristics of his prose.

Hernández gave to his prose its popular tone by employing a number of devices: the presentation of almost anonymous protagonists; the use of many Mexican words and phrases, such as *zentzontle, huacal, el cuete*, and *un petate de estrado*; allusions to various historical and political events and personages, as well as descriptions of the masses and of their reactions; the *sanchesco* inclusion of many proverbs and popular sayings: "Nunca dejes camino real por vereda"; "Sabe más el diablo por viejo que por diablo"; "No hay mal que se padezca por cien años"; "De los parientes y el sol, mientras más lejos mejor." His prose abounds with antitheses and paradoxes, which are usually treated in a humorous tone. He can find almost too easily parallels between opposites. The short story, "Un escritor muy bien agradecido" begins:

> No comenzaré hablando del día, ni en toda la historia me ocuparé de él, porque voy a tratar asuntos que acaecieron de noche.
> No hablaré tampoco de la noche, porque mis ojos no tienen la virtud de los del murciélago.

In the same story he wrote: "Solía llover en el tiempo de las aguas. Solía llover en el tiempo de secas, pero, en general, llovía más en el tiempo de aguas que en el otro." [42] In "El señor de palo," Domingo has no difficulty in finding a close relationship between the Bible and economic history. God

[42] *Obras*, 290–91.

became angry at Adam and Eve, who were in hiding because of shame for their nakedness. Therefore, they decided to clothe themselves; and "en esta anécdota comienza la historia de las fábricas de hilados y tejidos." [43]

In his prose one finds frequent use of Latin phrases and Church terms, as well as legal words and phrases. These learned expressions are not there to obfuscate, but rather to add to the humorous and the ironical tone. For the same purpose he mentions the names of great historical, literary, and religious figures. In writing of Christ when he ran the money-changers from the temple, Hernández describes him as "un señor tan apacible como éste, que sólo se enojó una vez, la vez que se enojó en la Lagunilla." [44] Both the wit and the irony here depend on the fact that, in Mexico City, the Lagunilla, the market place, is also called the Thieves' Market. Such examples of humor permeate his prose works. Santa Teresa, he wrote, cannot be a saint, because "yo tengo el honor de conocerlas [santas] personalmente, y santas son unas señoras que no se mueven nunca, que permanecen quietecitas en los nichos de los templos, o bajo los capelos de cristal en los rinconeras de las casas." [45]

In "Un escritor muy bien agradecido," he reasons humorously from a false premise to the logical conclusion "that the Royal Academy does not know grammar." He deplores the prevailing ignorance of the higher classes of Mexico when he observes: "Afortunadament aquí hay autores clásicos, mejores que el Bromural para el insomnio." [46] And at times his humor becomes bitter, as when he confronts the relativity of life with his concept of the realm of the absolute.

There is much satire of a *humorístico* type directed against the religious, political, educational, and social

[43] *Ibid.*, 33.
[44] *Ibid.*, 284.
[45] *Ibid.*, 285.
[46] *Ibid.*, 284.

spheres "en este país tan bello como sin esperanza . . ." [47]
He bemoaned especially the lack of humility in the political
world; and he pictured the arrogance, the laziness, the in-
efficiency, and the dishonesty of officials of government,
from the very petty ones to "su excelencia, el señor minis-
tro, que hablaba a diario con el señor presidente ... ." The
great lack in his country, he felt, was the natural humility
which is the result of true intelligence. "Es claro," he wrote,
"a más inteligencia corresponde más asombro, no menos mis-
terio; pero, entre todos, aquel que más se abisma es el que
pesa menos." [48]

Although there are more figures of speech to be found
in Hernández's prose than in his poetry, both are filled with
subtle and delicate metaphors, similes, personifications, and
apostrophes. It is the metaphor which is the most important
of these figures of speech in Hernández's work. There are
the simple metaphors, such as a description of storm clouds
as "naves de acero de la mar de los aires." [49] The greater
number of the metaphors, however, are presented in terms
of personification. Time, for example, may be a clock on
which the hours flee, "eternities of bitterness among thorns."
Or time may be personified, when, at its death:

> ... el tiempo, su frente de cansancio,
> sus alas doloridas
> y sus pies sin reposo,
> vuelva, al fin, a la casa de sus padres.[50]

Similes, though less frequent than metaphors, are equally
subtle, equally delicate and sometimes comical:

Una nubecita ... similar al algodón Johnson and Johnson ... como
una pequeña ilusión. ...

47 *Ibid.,* 257.   49 *Ibid.,* 286.
48 *Ibid.,* 265.   50 *Ibid.,* 53.

... y el consuelo que sucede a las lágrimas vertidas, como candor, limpieza, blancura, que aparece por virtud lavandera del rocío.

... el amor es un paseo, ir del brazo con una incansable señorita, sin acabar nunca de andar, como hace el tiempo.

El silencio era una cosa que caía, que colgaba, como una cabellera de seda resbalando en los hombros de la noche de luna.[51]

Apostrophes, fewer yet, are to be found in the poetry, as when the writer addresses himself to the angel of sleep:

> Profundísimo ángel a quien amo
> desde tantas heridas,
> a quien clamo,
> desde tantas heridas.
>
> Príncipe de las vagas, incoloras,
> secretísimas ondas insensibles.
>
> Remero de las sombras
> congénere incruento de la muerte,
> nauta de los abismos, silencioso,
> suavísimo señor: ... [52]

Examples of onomatopoeia are sprinkled throughout the prose:

La llave goteaba: tastás, tastás, tastás.

... los patos que nadan ... todo el día cuá, cuá. ...

... un gallo muy falto de consideraciones dijo que quiquiriquí. ...

Cantaba el pajarito, ufifí, u fifí ... u fiiiii. ...

Pirí, pirí, cantaba con el pensamiento, como un gendameril silbato. ...[53]

Repetition is also a distinctive feature of Hernández's style. It involves not only adjectives but also nouns, ad-

[51] *Ibid.*, 120, 232, 285, 292.
[52] *Ibid.*, 64.
[53] *Ibid.*, 261, 278, 294, 318, 321.

verbs, phrases, and even whole clauses. Certain vocabulary clusters run through many of his poems and much of his prose almost like a leitmotiv:

> He aquí, yo sé quién eres,
> mejor que mis tristezas te conozco ...

> Ah del que murmurando
> palabras de rumor. ...

> Lo barato es caro. ...

> Landa callada y quieta, landa sola,
> pacífica y vacía. ...

Amor, amor. Tiene que ser amor. A amor teníamos que encontrar. ...

Él, no era sino un hombre. Un hombre no es sino la dos mil-millonésima parte de la humanidad. Y la humanidad es tan insignificante que, sin telescopio, no se puede ver desde la luna.

Derechito corrí, derechito, derechito. ...[54]

One of the most Mexican of the characteristics of Hernández's literary works lies in his use of diminutives, a device which is in keeping with the "diminutive" importance of his characters. Many examples of this device have already appeared in the quoted material. The use of the diminutive forms of nouns, adjectives, and adverbs—*toditito*, *ahorita*, *derechito*—is commonplace, just as it is in the everyday speech of Mexico. Also, the diminutive forms of proper names appear frequently; and occasionally, Hernández uses this form of the past participle: "Desde acá se veía, sentadito en el suelo." [55]

Despite the recurrent presence of popular elements in his prose, however, he easily combines elegant words with those of everyday speech: "... sus efímeros ojos fueron como pe-

[54] *Ibid.*, 10, 12, 19, 21, 41, 43, 44, 258, 301, 362.
[55] *Ibid.*, 413.

rrenes prados tempraneros, anegados, como ondeantes va-
lles ..." [56] He knew how to describe the sky in philosophical terms and how to make a barren landscape come to life
with eloquence. Through extended comparisons, he verbally
united landscape and the characters of his stories and novels.

His sense of place seems stronger than his sense of time.
Although he chose as the locale for his novel, *La paloma, el
sótano y la torre*, the provincial area of his birth, the locale
for the greater part of his stories is Mexico City and its en-
virons. The note of nostalgia which pervades his works
grows out of the fact that the action always takes place in
the past, and often in the very indefinite past. It springs,
also, from the yearning which, throughout his adult life,
the writer continued to feel for his early home. Even the
sky was different there, was clearer, more transparent:

De cierto, no sé qué cosa tiene el cielo aquí [Mexico City]
que transparenta el universo a través de un velo de tristeza.

Allá [Guanajuato] son muy raras las tardes como ésta, casi
siempre se muestra el cielo transparente, teñido de un maravi-
lloso azul, que no he encontrado nunca en otra parte alguna.
Cuando empieza a anochecer, se ven en su fondo las estrellas,
incontables, como arenitas de oro bajo ciertas aguas que tienen
privilegios de diamante.[57]

Rosario Castellanos gives a comprehensive description of
Hernández's protagonists, or "habitante del universo." He is
an irresponsible innocent, never serious, never able to dominate circumstances, never triumphing over others, one who
often wanders through ruins on his solitary night walks.[58]
Hernández pointed out that "por la noche todo es más
grande que a la luz. Sólo nosotros somos más pequeños, es-
tamos más perdidos." [59] This hero lacks practical sense and,

[56] *Ibid.*, 256.
[57] *Ibid.*, 297.
[58] Castellanos, "La obra de Efrén Hernández," *El Día*, March 3, 1963, 1.
[59] *Obras*, 301.

therefore, is poor. He lacks aggression and material pride and is disdainful of his social insignificance. He neither inspires respect, solicits our sympathy, nor makes us want to laugh at him. Because he is filled with a very subtle malice, he hurries to laugh at himself and then at us. Names, circumstances, and events change, but this innocent protagonist remains constant. He excites in the reader tenderness and sympathy.

Few of the characters bear such imposing names as Cato (Catito); more often their own anonymity extends even to such names as Fulán (John Doe) or Abarca (a peasant's sandal). In spite of his anonymity, however, this "inocente" is not taken from the faceless masses. He is always the possessor of certain moral, cultural, and social values, but these are not stated in an obvious way. Hernández explained that nobody knows much about this "hero," because "nadie se ocupó de investigar sus cosas. Distinto hubiera sido, si este muchacho, en vez de ser un pobre diablo, hubiera sido Napoleón o un hueso de tetrabeladonte." [60] He explained, also, that "como no tenía ambición, era uno de esos que cantan mucho." [61] This statement he used as a stepping stone toward satirizing the social situation, with all its selfishness and egocentricity.

There are two types of men, Hernández insisted: those dedicated to *caridad* or *egoísmo*, to *generosidad* or *ruindad*, to *ofrecer* or *pedir*. And, he added, it is equally true for rich and poor alike. Out of the anguish of life, he believed, comes "el cantar en grande, de los grandes; de allá, el anhelo de huir, de dormir, de los pequeños ... ." [62]

At times, Hernández refuses to "seguir en pormenor los largos y hondos hilos" of the development of a character, "porque por este proceso hemos pasado ya personal-

[60] *Ibid.,* 290–91.
[61] *Ibid.,* 137.　　　　　　[62] *Ibid.,* 253.

mente." [63] In truth, the reader often sees himself in the protagonist and lives the events in the story vicariously. He may hear once more the noises of the trains of yesteryear and see again in his mind's eye the little candy-filled glass pistols and the other treasures hawked by the "butcher boys." Suddenly he may find himself in step with the protagonist, as he shortens or lengthens his stride, trying to avoid stepping on the cracks in the sidewalk. Just as quickly he may find himself seeing in memory once more the beautiful and colorful reflections in the soap bubbles of his childhood.

The subcharacters are occasionally well delineated. More often, however, they represent abstractions—justice, energy, fear of authority, resignation, maternal love—rather than people with lives of their own.

The poetic mixture of poetry in prose, both in word and in thought, indicates stylistically the mutability of life itself, the unity between the psychic and the physical parts of man. Therefore, the true hero is usually on a symbolic plane; and descriptions, not actions, are most important. In all the work of Hernández, this hero, this *inocente*, is *man*, the frail creature imprisoned *entre apagados muros*, who must choose between the *sótano* and the *torre*.

The short novel, *Cerrazón sobre Nicomaco* (1946), is considered as superior in some ways to the longer *La paloma* (1949). Teresa Bosque Lastra affirms that, although the latter is more polished, it lacks the spontaneity and profundity of *Cerrazón*.[64] She feels that, at times, in the longer novel the author's search for the right word is obvious, and that he thus interrupts the spontaneous flow of the story. As an example of this trait she quotes the following paragraph:

"A la acción en que consiste la advertencia de esta úlcera, sucederá de inmediato un sentimiento de comiseración, el cual

---

[63] *Ibid.*, 159.
[64] Bosque Lastra, 67.

será tanto más profundo cuanto con más profundidad. Y ante este conocimiento, ante esta contemplación, el sufrimiento seco, duro, impío se humedecerá, se ablandará, se hará misericorde y, redimiéndose por los ojos, nos procurará tal alivio que, si una sola vez lo comprobamos, va en adelante nunca más dejaremos de acudir a este remedio." [65]

Another criticism aimed at *La paloma*, . . . is that the language spoken by the characters is too erudite for the social milieu he is depicting. While in a literal sense this is a valid criticism, one might argue that there is justification for the type of language used. The story is being told years later by Catito, who had been exposed in his youth to the language of his father, an educated man, and who in later life has evidently become an educated man himself. Little of the conversation is truly spoken; rather, much of it is recounted by the third person, Catito. Furthermore, much of it proceeds from within—the oneiric state—a sublimated condition which Hernández seemed to feel was above and beyond the reach of the everyday grammar and choice of words within the grasp of the social group concerned. To him this condition could best be portrayed in a poetic manner, thus he used the combination of popular and more polished words. A further justification lies in the fact that the shorter novel delineates the failure of one life, while the longer sets forth the mutability of life itself and the emerging unity of the psychic and the corporeal parts of man. In the latter work, then, there is the calculated mixture of prose and poetry that one finds, for example, in Rilke's *Aufzeichnungen des Malte Laurids Brigge*.

In his desire for perfection of style, Hernández polished and repolished his work, seeking for such harmony of word, of thought, of rhythm that nothing might disturb the clear reflection of what he sought to project. To do less would

[65] *Obras*, 121; quoted by Bosque Lastra, 67.

have contradicted the message of his words and the obvious intent of his poetic mission. While an analysis of style must, at one point or another, deal with choice of vocabulary, figures, devices, and narrative techniques, there remains the trenchant point concerning Hernández's style: It was to him more than a means of expression; it was the reflection of his philosophical and emotional physiognomy. It had to blend the cosmic opposites that constituted the matter of his work. If the stylistic merging of these opposites seems at times somewhat strained, then the reader must recognize, also, that the merging of the things of this world and the reality of the ideal realm is a gigantic task, one that Hernández did not abjure.

Chapter VI

NOTES ON THE CUENTOS

THE APPEARANCE of the short story, "Tachas," in 1928, made the public aware of the literary personality and style of Efrén Hernández. Because of the autobiographical flavor of this story, he became known among his friends as Tachas, and this nickname was to go with him throughout the rest of his life. All of his prose work and especially the *cuentos* were of such autobiographical nature that, indeed, he might as correctly have been called by the name of any one of his protagonists. He and they *were* one.

In each of the stories the protagonist is a natural dreamer. Whenever reality touches him he tries to pull himself away from the dream long enough to face it, to pose some question, and then he returns to the dream. Typically, in his musings, he takes the common, everyday occurrence and associates it with some esthetic ideal, some philosophical or psychological concept, or, perhaps, a combination of the three.

Critics and reviewers have written about Hernández's *cuentos* with a tone of admiration that sometimes seems distressingly uniform. Gilberto González y Contreras states that nobody has written and sung in such poetic prose, "the experiences within the dream, that are, in reality, experiences within the soul." [1] More than characters, he feels, Hernández created personalized situations; and more than actions, thoughts—"allegories of impalpable realism." Hernández is praised by another critic for having taken his materials from the everyday world and changed them subtly into "a special reality between the poles of comedy and mystery." [2] He is described as having dedicated himself to serving his peculiarly poetic imagination, one which like a flood "flows without ceasing, always seeking its level, overcoming all obstacles and resistance." [3] "Tachas" is supposed to be a microcosm of the essence of Mexico.[4]

The idea for "Tachas" came from an event during Hernández's student days. Dr. Pascual Aceves Barajas, a longtime family friend, in relating the circumstances of this incident, writes that it took place during a class in philosophy at the University of Mexico. The professor called on Hernández for the answer to a question. And suddenly, Hernández returned from some dream world to realize that the professor was addressing him. "So help me God, Señor," he said, "you caught me when I wasn't paying attention." The professor, filled with the ideas of the positivism of Comte and Barreda, was shocked at the idea of calling upon God. "Mr. Hernández, we live in an epoch of realities and of the investigation of truth. We must believe only in what we can see, in what we can feel, in what has tangible reality. In short, we can only believe in what we can prove." Hernández, who, according to Dr. Aceves, was a good Catholic

---

[1] Gilberto González y Contreras, "Efrén Hernández: Poeta del cuento," *Mañana*, March 29, 1948, 72.

[2] José Luis Martínez, "Vida literaria en México: Poetas jóvenes," *ibid.*, November 20, 1943, 56.

[3] Rosario Castellanos, 1–2.

[4] Rubén Salazar Mallén, "La muerte de Efrén Hernández," 3; A. Quintero Álvarez, "Efrén Hernández," *Hoy*, July 15, 1939, 92.

because of his early training, answered him somewhat disrespectfully in a disgusted tone. The professor immediately became angry. But Efrén tried to console him by telling him, "Don't get so upset, Professor, it is only necessary to believe in tangible evidence, and what I have just said is not tangible." [5]

The setting for "Tachas" is the same, except that the incident takes place in a class dealing with law. The little story presents a polemic between reason (the law professor) and imagination (the student). The student is rudely pulled from his daydream back into the world of reality when he suddenly realizes that the professor is addressing him with the question: "¿Qué cosa son tachas?" His efforts to find the correct definition serve as the pretext for his mental wanderings as he proceeds to give a catalogue of the meanings the word has in Mexico. He even includes the feminine nickname, Tachas. Each definition leads to other digressions. The most humorous touch grows out of the fact that the one meaning which he cannot define is the pertinent, legal one, the only one in which the professor is interested.

In this autobiographical story, the students in the class bear the real names of college friends of Hernández. And, in the sentence, "Todos se rieron, menos el Tlacuache y yo, que no somos de este mundo," [6] he probably refers to the writer, César Garizurieta, who, by the time that the story was written, had died.[7]

This story seems simple enough on the surface, even as all of the *cuentos* are casually entertaining. But the *aficionados* of Hernández will recognize here the same themes that dominate the poetry, the essays, and the more difficult passages of the novels. Indeed, the stories can be read and

---

[5] Aceves Barajas, "Vida, consagración y ausencia de Efrén Hernández," 1–10.

[6] *Obras*, 281.   [7] See Bosque Lastra, 36.

enjoyed by the uninitiated, but they pose more difficulty in understanding than do the other genres.

The gap between plot and ultimate meaning is more obvious in "Santa Teresa," which relates the musings of a young student in the privacy of his bedroom during an overnight visit in the country home of Don Maurilio. The latter does not understand the tragedy of his young daughter's sufferings from the frustrations of her isolated life. In this story are to be found elements of the fable, religious and political satire, and doubt. The philosophical quality grows out of the student's musings, while the psychological quality lies in the frustrated sex urge within the daughter, which frustration is only hinted at in the biting of her fingernails and in such veiled allusions as the following: "Inés, ¿porqué no cenas?" asks her father. "Pero ella estaba pensando en una golondrina que dio un tope contra un campanario y se quebró." [8]

In "Un escritor muy bien agradecido," there is bitter, but always humorous, satire concerning the public's lack of appreciation of the dedicated writer. Here again is a polemic between imagination and reality, with a justification of imagination which flows freely, "deslizándose por una pendiente resbaladiza . . ." [9] In this short story, which delineates a dream sequence followed by the period of awakening, the author very subtly plants in the mind of the reader the question: Which, in truth, is the dream? Once again, Hernández emphasizes his belief that in this world all is relative. Here he also points out his deep respect for human life:

> Lo veis: La vida podrá ser deleznable, pero es hermosa.
> Moraleja:
> Debemos: no atentar contra la vida. [10]

Once again here is the element of the fable.

[8] *Obras,* 289.　　　　[9] *Ibid.,* 310.　　　　[10] *Ibid.,* 303.

"El señor de palo," one of his finest short stories, has been so often mentioned in this study that it will suffice here to point out only its over-all theme: *Quietismo*, or the suppressing and the overcoming of all desire. "Un clavito en el aire" is a philosophical story concerning the search for a concise definition of time. The main source of humor grows out of his manner of deductive reasoning, involving a specious syllogism:

> *Lo barato es raro*
> *Lo raro es caro*
> luego *Lo barato es caro.*[11]

The plot is simple. The protagonist, while delving into the metaphysical problem of the meaning of time, claims to have been on the verge of an all-encompassing definition. Then suddenly the door, the cheap wood of which has become water soaked during the rainy season, is split open by the drying process of the hot sun. A strong draft rushes in and blows his hat off his head; and he, in the effort to recover the hat, loses his train of thought, never to regain it.

"Incompañía" emphasizes the tragedy of the inability to feel unselfish love and of an inflated feeling of self-importance in this imperfect world. The musings grow out of the death of a dog and the subsequent dumping of its body into a garbage can. Then, when the garbage can is dumped into the city garbage truck, the only thing which remains in the can is a straw.

¡Ay! ya veis qué cosa más insignificante es un popote; pues todos, en esta vida, hemos de acabar por perder nuestra importancia y descender a tan insignificantes como un fragmento de popote. Y quién sabe cuantos no lo seamos ya, y yo más que ninguno; pero no me olvidéis, que mirad si os amo, que sólo con el deseo de distraeros y de hacer menos graves vuestros días de

[11] *Ibid.*, 341.

ocio y soledad, he estado escribiendo este pequeño escrito sentimental, ridículo e implacable. ...[12]

Hernández, who, like Nietzsche and Sudermann, was strongly attracted by the mysteries of the mechanisms of conduct, with all their complexities, treats of this subject in "Sobre causas de títeres." This little story deals principally with the tenuous and difficult balance which must be maintained between the world of imagination and dreams and the practical world around us. For one who has read Hernández's poetry, the following excerpt should demonstrate that beneath the facile delineation of the story are the same philosophical problems that informed the poetic style of the man:

> Ya, viejo, ya muy cierto es que no estamos en edad de soñar sueños de niños; pero estamos en ello, tan lejos como cerca de nosotros, vamos por la pendiente resbalosa y luciente de los sueños, y el peligro de resbalar sin caer, patinando de pie, hacia atrás, sin objeto a do asirse y para abajo, es infinito. ...[13]

In "Unos cuantos tomates en una repisita" Serenín, the protagonist, is led to the evidence of the unity of all things. Here again the reasoning is through a humorous and spurious type of logic, and Hernández cites Pascal:

> Con cuanta razón ha sido dicho: "Tiene el corazón sus razones que la razón no conoce." Caminando de ecuación en ecuación, de semejanza en semejanza. Serenín ha llegado a demostrar, casi nada, sólo que el agujero este, y el cielo, son lo mismo.[14]

In this story there is a very good example of Hernández's presentation of psychological themes. Although he never mentions Pavlov or the fact that he is alluding to the conditioned reflex, he manages to present the meaning of it in humorous incidents such as this one involving Serenín. He relates that Serenín as a child had once been forced by his

[12] *Ibid.*, 349.   [13] *Ibid.*, 355.   [14] *Ibid.*, 370.

father to take off his clothes and go out into the wind and the rain; and as a result of this, Serenín had pneumonia. Forever after, he feared even to open a window; and whenever he felt a draft, he put "mentolato en las ventanas de la nariz ... ."

"Una historia sin brillo" emphasizes the great value of true, unselfish love between the sexes. "Don Juan de las Pitas habla de la humildad," more a philosophical essay than a *cuento*, deals with the true meaning of humility. Here, reminiscent of Unamuno, Hernández treats of the various *yo*'s ("I's") of the individual: the *yo* which the world sees, the *yo* which the individual thinks he is, and the *yo* which the individual really is. Once again, in "Carta tal vez de más," he presents a polemic between faith and reason. A friend has appealed to the hero to help her in her dilemma. The protagonist tries to apply the scientific method and to reason to a logical conclusion with words. But in using words, he finds that he must depart from the concrete in speaking of the abstract. He compares it to a stairway, with the lowest part a concrete thing and the highest part—the concept, the spirit—hidden in the heights, out of sight. He still holds to his position on the side of reason:

> Ni un truco ni un descuido. Muy cierto es que parece ser así, pero en caso de serlo no ha sido un truco mío, ha sido un truco del idioma. Y en mi humilde concepto no constituye falla. Se debe sólo a un acto de obediencia y disciplina en que la realidad se impone a la mentira que es toda ficción, así sea la muy científica y matemática llamada regla de falsa posición.[15]

He continues to assure the friend that he will stay with his reasoning until he can give her a logical and true answer. But throughout the story the philosophical currents beneath the surface indicate the true meaning of the story: One

---

[15] *Ibid.*, 399.

cannot find God through logic; it is logic (science) which took God away.

"Trabajos de amor perdidos" presents a little picture of childhood days and once again underscores the picaresque qualities of the young protagonist. "Toñito entre nosotros" points the way to overcoming "the coldness within the soul" [16] by realizing that everything in this world, be it happy or sad, is relative and finally passes.

The short stories, like the other works of Hernández, demonstrate that in his thoughts and sentiments, with their mystical quality of emotion, there was always evident, whether expressed or unexpressed, a deep and altruistic appreciation of and affection for his fellow man. It is this feeling to which he alludes in the last paragraph of "Tachas":

> Ya estoy en la calle, la llovizna cae, y viendo yo la manera como llueve, estoy seguro de que a lo lejos, perdido entre las calles, alguien, detrás de unas vidrieras, está llorando porque llueve así.[17]

It is not the object of this chapter to analyse the stories. Hernández, to the degree that he is a well-known writer today, already carries the designation *cuentista*, and, as such, is recognized by a great number of the commentators listed in the bibliography. The point is that the stories constitute yet another mode of expression for the poetic attitudes of the man, that their subtlety is philosophical, as well as psychological and humorous, and that their simplicity is deceptive. They also constitute a further proof that this ever paradoxical writer, while emphasizing the importance of reason, of intelligence, as his conscious mind demanded, was, in truth, more nearly in accord with the idea expressed by Unamuno when the latter wrote:

> ¿Hay una filosofía española, mi don Quijote? Sí, la tuya, la

16 *Ibid.*, 405.   17 *Ibid.*, 150.

filosofía de Dulcinea, la de no morir, la de creer la verdad. Y esta filosofía no se aprende en cátedras ni se expone por lógico inductiva ni deductiva, ni surge de silogismos ni de laboratorios, sino surge del corazón.[18]

Various friends and critics have dedicated to Hernández tributes both in poetry and prose setting forth the belief that along this path of love he finally reached his goal, a belief summed up in these words reminiscent of Hernández's own poetic work:

Incommunicado dentro de la propia necesidad de alcanzar la fe, logra el amor que lo salvará de la muerte "entre apagados muros," mismo título de su excelente libro.[19]

---

[18] Unamuno, *Vida de don Quijote y Sancho, según Miguel de Cervantes Saavedra*, 234.

[19] Frank Dauster, *Breve historia de la poesía mexicana*, 170.

BIBLIOGRAPHY

THE WORKS OF EFRÉN HERNÁNDEZ

BOOKS

Cerrazón sobre Nicomaco. Mexico City: Imprenta Claridad, 1946.
Cuentos. Mexico City: Imprenta Universitaria, 1941.
Entre apagados muros. Mexico City: Imprenta Universitaria, 1943.
Hora de horas. "Friends of the Fable Series." Mexico City, 1936.
Obras: Poesía, novela, cuentos. "Mexican Letters." Mexico City: Fondo de Cultura Económica, 1965.
La paloma, el sótano y la torre. Mexico City: Secretaría de Educación Pública, 1949.
El señor de palo. Mexico City, Acento, 1932.
Sus mejores cuentos. Mexico City: Editorial Novaro, 1956.
Tachas. Mexico City: Secretaría de Educación Pública, 1928.

ARTICLES

"Algunos pensamientos que surgieron tratando de encontrar una definición de poesía," *El Libro y el Pueblo*, II (July–August, 1941), 11–16.
"Alusiones," *La República*, XV (October, 1949), 21.
"El angel del subsuelo," *Hoy*, July 15, 1939, 28.

"Carta a Alfredo Maillefert," *Letras de México*, November 15, 1937, 3.

"Carta a Enrique Guerrero," *Letras de México*, January 16, 1938, 3.

"Del surrealismo," *El Popular*, April 19, 1940, 3.

"Descarrilamiento," *El Popular*, April 27, 1940, 3.

"En defensa del verso," *Hoy*, February 25, 1949, 28, 70.

"Evocación de Horacio: Poema de Salomón de la Selva," *La República*, October 15, 1949, 20.

"La falta del mérito en el cine," *La República*, July 15, 1949, 25.

"Ficha biográfica," *El Popular*, April 3, 1955, 3, 6.

"Himnos a Himnos," *El Libro y el Pueblo*, XIV (July–August, 1941), 11.

"La incubación del héroe," *La República*, August 15, 1949, 13.

"Manojo de aventuras (Una página inedita): 'Incógnita es incógnita' " *Novedades*, January 28, 1962, 3.

"Paquines y paquitos," *Futuro*, I, No. 50 (April, 1940), 30–31, 48.

"Un reportazgo ejemplar," *Futuro*, I, No. 51 (May, 1940), 50–51.

"Sobre lo humano en la poesía," *América*, I, No. 21 (October, 1943), 30–32.

"Sumarísimo extracto de una definición," *América*, I, No. 60 (August, 1949), 45.

"Trenzas," *América*, I, No. 50 (August, 1946), 45–47.

"Versos de una especie hoy no muy gustada," *América*, I, No. 50 (August, 1946), 45–47.

REFERENCES

BOOKS

Alonso, Dámaso. *Poesía española.* Madrid: Espasa-Calpe, 1944.

Anderson Imbert, Enrique. *Historia de la literatura hispano-americana.* Vol. II: *Época contemporánea.* 1st ed. Mexico City: Fondo de Cultura Económica, 1961.

Arellano, Jesús. *Poetas jóvenes de México*. Mexico City: Biblioteca Mínima Mexicana, 1956.

Calderón, Correo. *Baltasar Gracián: Su vida y su obra*. Madrid: Editorial Grados, 1961.

Cardona Peña, Alfredo. *Recreo sobre las letras*. Mexico City: Ministerio de Educación Pública, 1961.

Carmen Millán, María del. *Literatura mexicana*. 2nd ed. Mexico City: Editorial Esfinge, 1963.

Casalduero, Joaquín. *Sentido y forma del Quijote (1605–1615)*. "Island Editions." Madrid: Arges, 1949.

Castro Leal, Antonio. *La poesía mexicana moderna*. "Letras Mexicanas." Mexico City: Fondo de Cultura Económica, 1953.

Cervantes Saavedra, Miguel de. *El ingenioso hidalgo don Quijote de la Mancha*. Ed. by F. Rodríguez Marín. 8 vols. 8th ed. "Castilian Classics." Madrid: Espasa-Calpe, 1964.

Dauster, Frank. *Breve historia de la poesía mexicana*. Mexico City: Ediciones de Andrea, 1956.

Diáz Canedo, Enrique. *Letras de México*. Mexico City: El Colegio de México, 1944.

Eliot, T. S. *The Complete Poems and Plays, 1909–1950*. New York: Harcourt, Brace, and World, 1962.

Ernst, Frederick. *Literatura del siglo xx*. New York: New York University Press, 1955.

García López, José. *Historia de la literatura española*. 7th ed. Barcelona: Editorial Vicens-Vives, 1962.

Gómez, Aurora Maura Ocampo de. *Literatura mexicana contemporánea: Bibliografía crítica*. Mexico City: Publicación privada, 1948.

González Peña, Carlos. *Historia de la literatura mexicana*. 8th ed. Mexico City: Ed. Porrúa, 1963.

González Ramírez, Manuel, and Torres Ortega, Rebeca. *Poetas de México*. Mexico City: Ed. América, 1945.

Gracián, Baltazar. *El Criticón*. 6th ed. "Austral Collection." Madrid: Espasa-Calpe, 1964.

Henríquez Ureña, Pedro. *Las corrientes de la América-his-*

pánica. "Biblioteca Americana." Mexico City: Fondo de Cultura Económica, 1960.

Leal, Luis. *Bibliografía del cuento mexicano.* Mexico City: Ediciones de Andrea, 1958.

————. *Breve historia del cuento mexicano.* Mexico City: Ediciones de Andrea, 1956.

————. *Breve historia del cuento mexicano.* Part II: *Antología del cuento.* Mexico City: Ediciones de Andrea, 1957.

León, Fray Luis de. *Poesías completas.* Vol. I. 2nd ed. Buenos Aires: Editorial Sopena Argentina, 1942.

Lerín, Manuel, and Millán, Marco Antonio. *Veinte y nueve cuentistas mexicanos actuales.* Mexico City: Ed. América, 1945.

Madariaga, Salvador de. *Guía del lector del Quijote: Ensayo psicológico sobre el Quijote.* 5th ed. Buenos Aires: Edicion Sudamericana, 1961.

Mancisidor, José. *Cuentos mexicanos de autores contemporáneos.* Mexico City: Editorial Nueva Espana, 1946.

Martínez, José Luis. *Literatura mexicana del siglo xx (1910–1949).* Mexico City: Antigua Librería Robleda, 1950.

Millán, Marco Antonio, and Lerín, Manuel. *Veinte y nueve cuentistas mexicanos.* Mexico City: Ed. América, 1945.

Murry, John Middleton. *El estilo literario.* Mexico City: Ediciones de Andrea, 1960.

Pradal-Rodríguez, Gabriel. *Antonio Machado (1875–1939): Obra y vida—Bibliografía—Antología—Obra inédita.* Intro. by Federico de Onís. Hispanic Institute in the United States. New York: Casa Hispánica of Columbia University, 1951.

Rojas Garcidueñas, José. *Breve historia de la novela mexicana.* Mexico City: Ediciones de Andrea, 1959.

Torres Ortega, Rebeca, and González Ramírez, Manuel. *Poetas de México.* Ediciones de Andrea, 1959.

Torres-Rioseco, Arturo. *Ensayos sobre la literatura hispanoamericana.* Mexico City: Fondo de Cultura Económica, 1958.

Turnbull, Eleanor L., ed. *Ten Centuries of Spanish Poetry*. Baltimore: Johns Hopkins Press, 1955.

Unamuno, Miguel de. *Del sentimiento trágico de la vida*. "Contemporary Library." Buenos Aires: Editorial Losada, 1964.

————. *En torno al casticismo*. Madrid: 1895.

————. *Vida de don Quijote y Sancho, según Miguel de Cervantes Saavedra*. 8th ed. Buenos Aires: Espasa-Calpe, 1949.

Valbuena Prat, Ángel. *Historia de la literatura española*. Vol. II. 6th ed. Barcelona: Editorial Gustavo Gili, 1960.

Valenzuela, Alberto. *Novelistas de México*. Mexico City: Ábside, 1959.

ARTICLES AND THESIS

A.R.C. "Entre apagados muros," *Así*, June 12, 1943, 33.

"Ábside cumple dieciocho años," *La Nación*, November 28, 1954, 19.

Aceves Barajas, Pascual. "Vida, consagración y ausencia de Efrén Hernández," *El Universal Gráfico*, March 2, 1958, 1, 10.

Alday, Francisco. "Poesía inédita: 'El ángel del sueño,'" *La Nación*, February 9, 1958, 33.

Andrade, Gonzalo Alfredo. "Un intento de concepción de un universo," *Nosotros*, September 3, 1949, 36–37.

Avilés, Alejandro. "Efrén Hernández, el hombre," *El Universal Gráfico*, November 16, 1926, 17.

————. "Efrén no ha muerto. ¿No ves que está jugando?" *La Nación*, February 2, 1958, 35.

————. "Poetas del siglo xx," *Señal*, I (January, 1954), 7.

Barba Jacob, Porfirio. "El hombre y su obra," *Novedades*, January 28, 1962, 1, 3.

Blanco, Octavio. "El libro de la quincena: Entre apagados muros," *Tiras de Colores*, July 16, 1943, 9.

Bonifaz Nuño, Alberto. "El cuentista, Efrén Hernández," *Novedades*, March 23, 1952, 2–3.

Bonifaz Nuño, Rubén. "Efrén Hernández," *Novedades*, March 23, 1953, 3.

———. "Efrén Hernández," *Novedades*, March 30, 1952, 2.

Bosque Lastra, Teresa. "La obra de Efrén Hernández." Master's thesis, Universidad Iberoamericana, 1963.

Bustamente, Octavio. "A la carta: 'Carta a Efrén Hernández,' " *El Universal Gráfico*, April 3, 1948, 6.

———. "A la carta: 'Carta a Efrén,' " *El Universal Gráfico*, March 5, 1949, 10.

———. "A la carta: 'Homenaje a Tachas,' " *El Universal Gráfico*, May 21, 1949, 6.

———. "Efrén Hernández," *América*, I, No. 20 (June, 1941), 7.

———. "Efrén Hernández," *El Universal Gráfico*, May 3, 1941, 7.

C.N. "Ocho poetas mexicanos," *La Nación*, December 19, 1954, 18.

"La cabeza de pájaros," *Así*, February 1, 1941, 54.

Carballo, Emanuel. "Estatismo y digresión," *Novedades*, January 6, 1957, 2.

Cardona Peña, Alfredo. "Espejo de la voz: Efrén Hernández," *Novedades*, October 24, 1943, 2.

Castellanos, Rosario. "La obra de Efrén Hernández," *El Día*, March 3, 1963, 1–2.

Cortés Tamayo, Ricardo. "Con el lápiz suelto," *La Prensa Gráfica*, January 12, 1946, 7.

———. "El retrato," *El Día*, March 3, 1963, 2.

Cruz Garciá, Salvador de la. "La paloma, el sótano y la torre," *Fuensanta*, I (March, 1949), 4.

D.F. "Cantinflas tiene a su alcance el argumentista que necesita," *Mañana*, February 1, 1950, 11.

Dalevuelta, Jacobo. "Efrén Hernández: 'La paloma, el sótano y la torre,' " *El Universal*, April 17, 1949, 5.

"De la república de los mexicanos," *Presente*, January 12, 1946, 12.

"La disciplina escolástica ... las inquietudes modernas," *Novedades*, January 11, 1948, 3.

Dueñas, Guadalupe. "El hombre y su obra," *Novedades*, January 28, 1962, 1, 3.

Echevarría del Prado, Vicente, and Galvez, Ramón. "Pausas literarias," *Novedades*, August 10, 1947, 5.

"Efrén Hernández," *Novedades*, January 11, 1948, 6.

"Efrén Hernández: Cuentos," *Letras de México*, July 14, 1941, 5.

"Efrén Hernández: El mejor prosista de México," *El Popular*, April 9, 1940, 3, 6.

"Exégesis: El poeta y la muerte ... Tránsito de Efrén Hernández," *El Zócalo*, January 30, 1958, 10.

"Fue sepultado ayer el gran prosista mexicano, Efrén Hernández: 'Tachas,'" *El Zócalo*, January 30, 1958, 3.

Galvez, Ramón, and Echevarría del Prado, Vicente. "Pausas literarias," *Novedades*, August 10, 1947, 5.

García Norezo, G. "Pequeño llanto por Efrén," *Novedades*, February 2, 1958, 3.

Garcidueñas, J. R. "Notas sobre tres novelas mexicanas," *Anales del Instituto de Investigaciones estéticas*, XVI (1943), 12.

González Contreras, Gilberto. "Efrén Hernández: Poeta del cuento," *Mañana*, March 29, 1948, 72.

Henestrosa, Andrés. "La nota cultural: Efrén Hernández," *El Nacional*, January 29, 1958, 3.

Hernández, M. "Reinventario de la producción hernandina," *El Libro y el Pueblo*, IV (September, 1963), 8.

Jarnés, Benjamín. "La trampa de una naturaleza muerta," *Hoy*, September 16, 1939, 55.

Lerín, Manuel. "Literatura en Efrén Hernández," *América*, I, No. 32 (December, 1944), 24, 25.

López Trujillo, Clemente. "Efrén Hernández, cuentista," *El Nacional*, October 18, 1941, 3.

Martínez, José Luis. "Vida literaria en México: Poetas jóvenes," *Mañana*, November 20, 1943, 56–57.

————. "Efrén Hernández," *Novedades*, July 8, 1962, 3.

Millán, Marco Antonio. "El fertil martirio de Efrén Hernández debe ser mejor estimado," *El Libro y el Pueblo*, IV (September, 1963), 1–5, 31.

————. "El hombre y su obra," *Novedades*, January 28, 1962, 3.

————. "Murió el 'Tachas' ... , " *El Zócalo*, February 2, 1958, 12.

————. "Efrén Hernández: Su inconformidad responsable y esperansada," *Novedades*, January 28, 1962, 3.

Mendoza, María Luisa. "Efrén el grande y el pequeño Hernández," *Excelsior*, March 17, 1957, 2–4.

Noriega, Raúl. "Breve historia del cuento en México," *Novedades*, January 8, 1962, 2–3, 6.

Novaro, Octavio. "Epinicio por Efrén," *El Día*, March 3, 1963, 2.

————. "Presencia de Efrén Hernández: Efrén Hernández o la inmodestia," *Novedades*, January 28, 1962, 3.

Ortiz Ávila, Raúl. "El ruiseñor y la prosa: 'Tachas,' " *El Nacional*, February 2, 1958, 3, 9.

Ortiz Paniagua, Ernesto. "Efrén, el poeta de la luz," *El Universal Gráfico*, August 3, 1952, 16, 20.

Pasquel, Leonardo. "El hombre y su obra," *Novedades*, January 28, 1962, 1, 3.

Poniatowska, Elena. "Tachas," *Novedades*, February 2, 1957, 3.

Quintero Alvárez, Alberto. "Efrén Hernández," *Hoy*, July 15, 1939, 92.

Rius Facius, Antonio. "Efrén Hernández," *Excelsior*, March 2, 1958, 2–3.

S.N.V. "La paloma, el sótano y la torre," *El Universal Gráfico*, March 8, 1949, 7, 20.

Salazar Mallén, Rubén. "Ocho poetas mexicanos," *El Universal*, January 9, 1955, 3.

————. "La muerte de Efrén Hernández," *El Universal Gráfico*, February 4, 1958, 3, 8.

Sotomayor, Arturo. "De que vive el escritor mexicano," *Novedades*, April 24, 1949, 2.

Tejera, Humberto. "Poemas epigramáticos de Efrén Hernández," *El Nacional*, December 18, 1949, 3, 6.

Tiquet, José. "Efrén Hernández: *Entre apagados muros*," *El Universal Gráfico*, August 31, 1951, 7.

————. "Efrén Hernández: El hombre y su obra," *Novedades*, January 28, 1962, 1, 3.

Valenzuela, Alberto. "Novelistas de México," *Ábside*, XXIII (April–June, 1959), 245–47.

Villaseñor, Raúl. "Tachas, el intachable," *Excelsior*, February 9, 1958, 3.

Villaurrutia, Xavier. "El señor de palo," *El Libro y el Pueblo*, X (December, 1932), 14–15.

————. "Efrén Hernández, el señor de palo," *Examen*, II (September, 1939), 24–25.

INDEX